MY DAYS IN PRISON

My Days in Prison

(*Kaaragaar*)

URMILA SHASTRI

Translated from the Hindi by
Sonal Parmar

With an introduction by
Kasturba Gandhi

HARPER
VANTAGE

First published in India in 2012 by Harper Vantage
An imprint of HarperCollins *Publishers*

Building 10, Tower A, 4th Floor, DLF Cyber City, Phase II,
Gurugram Haryana – 122002, India
www.harpercollins.co.in

2 4 6 8 10 9 7 5 3

P-ISBN: 978-93-5029-235-8
E-ISBN: 978-93-5029-462-8

Typeset in Perpetua 11/14.5
InoSoft Systems Noida

Printed and bound at
MicroPrints India, New Delhi

Contents

Foreword

Freedom at Midnight

Any Indian who lived through that era will recall the 'Tryst with Destiny' speech by Jawaharlal Nehru on August 14, 1947 as one of the greatest speeches ever made. Truly inspirational, it has the ability to move us even now, 65 years later.

Many of us do not realize that this freedom at midnight marked the end of a long period of slavery which had commenced at the Battle of Plassey over two centuries ago in 1757. This was the first time since then that India had won the battle for freedom.

Foreign nationals and armies had come to India throughout its recorded history from as early as 7th century B.C. For the most part, the newcomers, who cannot be termed as invaders stayed back to be absorbed by Bharatvarsh. The battle of Plassey was the first time a foreign power arrived in the disguise of a trading company and began ruling a part of India, only to extend its rule gradually to most of the subcontinent. Indian maharajas were permitted to rule their states as long as they owed allegiance to the British Crown. Their good behaviour was watched over by a British 'Resident'.

The attempt at freedom in 1857, which is called the 'First War of Independence' by Indians and the 'Sepoy Mutiny' by the British was 'easily quelled' as described by a contemporary British administrator. Other attempts at winning freedom through armed rebellion met similar fate.

Mohandas Karamchand Gandhi created the route for Civil Disobedience, first by breaking the Salt Law at the Dandi March, and later by boycotting British goods. Millions of Indian heeded his call, some in spirit, others by action. They bought British goods and then burned them publically, exhorting others to follow suit.

The author of *Karaagar* was one such woman who was a sincere follower of Mahatma Gandhi. She was arrested in Meerut for boycotting British liquor and goods and put to trial during which the British magistrate asked her to apologize so that he could acquit her. She chose to go to jail instead for six months. What she wrote of her jail days in this slim work brings that era alive to us today.

The name Gandhi has been a symbol of strength and stability for governance in India since 1947. No matter which political party rules the country, the foundations of stability laid by Gandhi-ji shall forever remain strong. The message of his inspiration continues to guide India.

Urmila Shastri went to jail again in the Quit India Movement of 1942, once again on a call by Mahatma Gandhi. This time she fell seriously ill and was denied proper treatment. She was released after serving her sentence. She died with a smile on her face. Her ideals and principles have been a source of inspiration to me, and even though she is no more, she continues to be a guiding light in my life.

The reprint of this book written by Urmila Shastri in 1930 will remind us of many who joined the march to that 'Tryst with Destiny'.

— Kamal Nath

Union Cabinet Minister for Urban Development

Introduction

I congratulate Urmiladevi Shastri on writing this beautiful book about her experiences in prison. After getting married she came to Meerut with the great hope of setting up a home with her husband. However, she soon left the bliss of her new life for the sake of her motherland, accepting to go to jail with a smile on her face. In this war for freedom, our other sisters across India made similar sacrifices; they did womankind proud by displaying exemplary patriotism.

This book will be reminiscent of life in a jail to our sisters who have been there. Those sisters who unlike Urmila did not have the good fortune of going to jail will feel a certain envy on reading this book. I know that those saffron sari-clad women who peacefully boycotted British goods and picketed liquor shops haven't suffered any less for being brave. These patriots have suffered such miseries that make the prison atrocities pale in comparison; I have been witness to those days.

Urmila has written this book in such simple Hindi and lucid style that I did not face any difficulty in reading it. So, I congratulate her again specially for that.

— Kasturibai Gandhi
Satyagrahashram
Sabarmati

1

Before Going to Prison

It was the sixteenth of July, 1930. I was making preparations to go to Kashmir. In those days, my companions in the Congress Committee at Meerut were participating in the Satyagraha movement in large numbers. It was only after working with them continuously for four months that I was finally able to take a two-month break from the demands of my post. With a heart filled with enthusiasm I imagined my beloved Kashmir, its spellbinding beauty floating before my eyes. Unable to wait any more than I absolutely had to, I had already worked out the details of my forthcoming holiday. Suddenly, I heard voices from the street – 'Professor Pyarelal Sharma has been arrested!'

Sharmaji was one of the most respected leaders of Meerut. I was in a bind: considering the new circumstances, what would be the best thing for me to do? On the one hand was the desire to meet my family, my brothers and sisters, to relax and laze around, with the cool, soothing breeze of the valley caressing my face; on the other was the prospect of hard work in the blazing sun, labour that was most likely to culminate in prison. Unable to decide, I closed my eyes in an attempt to achieve greater clarity of thought. It didn't work. I couldn't make up my mind. Just then, even as I was in the throes of my dilemma, Professorji, my husband, entered the room.

'So Urmila, have you made your decision yet?' he asked me. 'Think carefully. You have to make a choice. Between duty and peaceful rest, between country and family. Which will it be?' The way the question had been framed, something in the manner in which it had been put to me, tugged at my soul. The sense of responsibility triumphed over the desire for domestic indulgence, and my decision in response to the call of duty was made.

At around 4 p.m., I was lying in my room. Professorji was sitting next to me, engrossed in a newspaper he was reading. Suddenly a thought came to me. 'Let's go get ourselves photographed,' I suggested excitedly. He looked at me in surprise at the complete unexpectedness of the wish expressed, but recovering quickly answered in the affirmative. 'Certainly,' he said. 'If you want to go immediately we could go to Sadar. A very famous photographer named Mr Mehmood has a studio there.'

I asked for an appointment with him. A servant was sent to find out what time would be suitable for us to go over. We were asked to come right away.

I got dressed and soon we were on our way. As soon as I got on to the tonga, I saw Shanta walking towards our house. Shanta was one of the members of the Women's Satyagrahi Committee and a friend. I could see a notice detailing the boycott of foreign goods in her hand. Coming up to the tonga she asked, 'So, where are you off to, all dressed up?' Laughing, I replied, 'To the end of the earth. Want to come along?' Shanta smiled in response and got on to the tonga.

Mr Mehmood had been waiting for us. Three photographs were clicked. As we were returning we crossed three lorries full of policemen near the police station, with the DSP's car parked in front of them. 'It looks like the volunteers picketing liquor shops in Sadar are going to be arrested,' Professorji said. As if coming to life at his words, the lorries rolled on towards the marketplace. Looking at me with concern, my husband said, 'Urmila, tomorrow it will be your turn.'

'How do you know?' I asked.

'My heart says so,' he replied.

Laughing at his words, I looked at him in amusement and said, 'How interesting! Your heart certainly says the most unexpected things at the most unexpected moments, doesn't it?'

A huge crowd had collected at the Barfkhana field. Speeches congratulating Sharmaji on his arrest were being made with patriotic fervour. My heart whispered to me to join in the speeches. 'It might just be your last chance to do so,' it said. Walking up to the chairperson, Quazi Nizamuddinji, I told him that I too wanted some time to say what I wished as I might not get the opportunity to do so again. Nizamuddinji nodded. 'All right,' he said. 'Go ahead. Take as much time as you wish.'

Soon it was my turn to speak. I walked up to the podium, the field resounding with echoes of 'Mahatama Gandhi ki jai'. Touched by the fervour I witnessed, my words flowed effortlessly, belief and conviction suffusing each syllable I articulated. I still remember my concluding words: 'Who knows who will be arrested tomorrow?' I asked. 'Who knows whom the shining rays of tomorrow's sun will awaken with the golden chains of imprisonment and the sacrifices demanded of mother-love?' And as the next day dawned, the words spoken by me proved more accurate than I could have ever imagined.

My eyes opened as soon as the clock struck one. In the dark I could make out Professorji as he stood near the bed with my servant Govardhan next to him. 'What is the matter?' I asked him, sitting up in alarm. 'It's only one o'clock. Why are you awake at this hour?'

'You will be able to stay in this house only for a few more hours, Urmila,' he said. Even though I could not understand what he was saying, something in his tone instinctively made me sit up. Repeating my question I waited for an explanation. He told me that the police would arrive at the house to arrest me at five in the morning.

'All right,' I said slowly. And then, with the intention of getting my things together, I started walking down the stairs. Soon I had set aside the things I intended to take along with me. Professorji told me to get some sleep. 'Your things will be packed by the time you wake up,' he assured me. At around a quarter past four he woke me up. 'I think you should get ready now.'

I got up, bathed and readied myself. At exactly five o'clock a police lorry came and parked itself in a corner at the crossing near my house. It had four or five policemen and a sub-inspector in it. A car arrived and began to blow its horn at my gate. I could see the DSP sitting in it, all alone with his driver. A few people from the neighbourhood also arrived. Raising a slogan of 'Mahatama Gandhi ki jai' I walked up and got into the car. Professorji accompanied me till I reached the police station. Along the way people standing on the roadside handed me flowers and garlands; accepting those tokens of their affection I folded my hands and bid farewell to them.

After a while, the car carrying me came to halt at the entrance of the Meerut District Jail near Abdullahpur. Behind us the lorry that had been following us all the way also stopped. 'Quazi sahib is also being brought here,' the DSP told me. I stopped near the entrance to wait for him. As another police lorry came into view I could see him sitting in it surrounded by policemen. Saying goodbye to Professorji, both of us entered the prison gates. And then, as the doors closed behind us, I was separated from the world outside for a long time to come.

As soon as I stepped into prison the first thing they did was to search me. The three books that had been part of my luggage – two on development and one a simple collection of stories – were confiscated. I had also brought a spring charkha along with me that the warden took away. Professorji had given me a letter before I had left home that morning. Because of the way events unfolded, I had been unable to read it properly at that time and had put it into my purse to read at leisure and to keep with me. The jailor asked me to hand that over as well.

Shaking my head in refusal I said, 'This letter is from my husband. I will not hand this over to you.'

'In that case, if you've read it,' he answered, 'please tear it up. I cannot allow you to take it inside with you.'

Right then and there I tore my precious letter to pieces. Throwing away the bits of paper I turned around and without looking back started walking towards my ward. In the distance I could feel the small bits of paper scattering, drifting aimlessly in the wind.

2

First Day in Prison

During those days, women sentenced to more than six months' imprisonment were sent directly to the Central Jail because of which the female wards in district prisons were usually very small. In the Meerut Central Jail the women's ward lay in the corner of the jail premises, barred within another secondary wall. There was only one entrance to the ward that in turn was blocked by a gate made of thick iron bars. There were always two locks on the gate – one outside and the other that the lady warden of the prison locked from inside and kept the keys of. The keys of the first lock were kept in the main office.

It was in front of this very gate that I was brought and made to stand. The lady warden and another jail inmate, who wore a number and was carrying my luggage, were with me. The warden opened the lock from outside and clanged the gate till someone came and unlocked it from inside. The gate opened. Turning to me she said, 'Come on, this is where you have to live now.' I entered the ward without speaking. As soon as I was inside, both the locks were back in place and the keys in them turned without delay.

The sweeper was an elderly Christian woman who had been born into a Brahmin family. 'This woman is a Brahmin by birth,' I was told. 'If you wish you can take her help in cooking.'

In front of the entrance there was a long barrack. Sitting there, watching me with interest, were two young women, both of them prisoners. Their hair was open and the clothes they wore were filthy and torn.

The sweeper took me inside the barrack. There were seventeen mud slabs lined up. She kept my things on one of them. By now I had realized that for many months to come this place was to be my home.

I looked around. In the corner of the room was a toilet. With shock I realized that I would have to sleep and eat in the same place. It was difficult coming to terms with all I saw around me, but I had no option; there was nothing else I could have done. In a corner, six mud slabs away from the toilet I opened my bedding.

The women's barrack had six entrances, on all except one of which seven thick iron rods barred the way. This was the only one which remained open at all times, a source of great discomfort to the prisoners in summer and winter alike. During summer the scorching heat of the blazing sun and the dry and dust-laden loo would torture them and during winters the chilly breeze and rain would make them shiver and curl up against the freezing cold. In direct contrast to this, the open door was a great convenience to the prison officials. Through it they could carry on constant surveillance of the prisoners and keep an eye on whatever they did.

Having taken it all in, I spread my sheet and sat down on what was supposed to be my bed. Suddenly the glorious cry of 'Praise be to Mother India, Bharat mata ki jai' rang out and filled the prison. Startled, I sat up. How wonderful to hear this cry in prison! It did not take me long to figure out where it had come from – the political prisoners in the men's barrack had hailed Nizamuddinji's entry in their midst by raising the slogan. 'Quazi sahib is now with friends,' I thought to myself. He had been welcomed into prison by the united cry of hearts and voices filled with enthusiasm and love. And I? My welcome? I had been welcomed only by the silence of the walls around me; by a guardian wind that made sure the soft stirrings of breeze came to an abrupt halt.

I had no friends or companions.

There were two other women in my barrack. One had run away from home and the other had been imprisoned after a fight over the issue of religious conversion. She had been born into a Brahmin family, but a short while after her birth her father had converted to Islam. When she reached a marriageable age she was married off to a Muslim man who would often beat her up. Fed up with the entire situation she finally got remarried to a Hindu man and went through the shuddhi process reinstating her to Hinduism. Because of this second marriage, a fight broke out between the Hindu and Muslim communities in the area and the woman, who was held responsible for the flare-up, was sentenced to six months' imprisonment.

The two women approached me slowly. One of them asked me, 'What crime have you been punished for?' With a smile I replied, 'The crime of loving my mother.'

The women looked at each other, neither of them able to comprehend what I was saying.

A little while later I was given a black blanket and a mat. The mat was to lie on and the blanket to cover myself with. It had not even been an hour since my arrival when the doors started clanging again. The sweeper ran, the door was unlocked and the superintendent entered the barrack accompanied by the jailor. A smaller barrack with just six beds was emptied and then offered to me. Seeing that its condition was much worse than that of the earlier one, I declined the offer and said that I preferred staying where I was. This offer, far from being motivated by any concern for my comfort, was in fact purely politically motivated – because of my status as an 'A' class prisoner, arrangements had been made to keep me separate from the others. Although none of my other fellow agitators who were also political prisoners were present, even the general prisoners were to be kept away from me. The authorities it seems feared my influence.

An iron bed from the prison hospital was brought in for me. I was also given some fresh fruit and a quarter litre of milk that was to serve as breakfast. This having been done I was left to myself and the door leading outside closed once again.

I was feeling hungry by now and picked up an orange. But to my amazement, as I peeled it I saw a small letter concealed inside. The contents of the letter were as follows:

> Behenji, 18.7.30
> Greetings!
> All of us would like to congratulate you on coming to prison. Whenever you get a chance to leave the ward and go to the visitor's area please be sure to look towards the entrance of our ward. We want to welcome you even if we are limited to doing so only from behind our bars.
> We are,
> Your brothers in struggle, the prisoners of this jail.

In a little while the door to my ward opened again and I saw the warden enter with another prisoner who was carrying something on his head. That 'something' turned out to be a mattress. Unlike most other prisoners I had been given a mattress by the jail authorities. But as I was soon to find out, sleeping on it was no different from sleeping on a bed of pebbles. The coarse, dry hay used to feed cows and buffaloes was stuffed into covers of thin, poor quality cloth. After several attempts of spreading it on my 'bed' I realized it was useless – the hay would simply lump up and stick out in uncomfortable bits here and there. Somehow I spread my mat on the iron cot and managed to lay out the 'mattress' on it. I knew that the mattress had been brought from the prison hospital and I wanted to know what the patients there had to go through when they were made to lie on them. With this thought in mind I lay down on it. Aah! What torture those poor patients must have to face each time they lay on the mattresses. I could not remain lying for even a whole minute! Tiny pointed tips of straw stuck out of the thin cloth at the least of pressure and the mattress took on the form of the Sheshnaag, stinging needles into the bodies of those who dared to lie on it – a thousand bites from a thousand tongues.

Sitting up I removed the mattress. But even then my task became no easier. Big holes gaped through the iron bed which made it impossible to spread anything on it. Finally, after several unsuccessful attempts I decided to let the iron cot be and spread my mat on the slab of mud. I had not slept well the previous night. In any case, one tends to get tired with constant work. I now realized that my days of rest had arrived. That is why the government of the country has put me here, I joked to myself, 'to allow me the rest and sleep I would never have been able to get outside'.

I tried sleeping. It was the month of July and the sun had already risen quite high in the sky, making it unbearably hot. There was no way to block out the glaring, scorching rays that filled my cell. As a result, even after repeated attempts to sleep I was still awake. Born in the earthly paradise of Kashmir, each year I would make it a point to escape there during the intense summer of the plains. This was therefore my first real experience of summer; a summer I spent on the plains of India and that too in a prison cell where not just the heat but the relentless attack of innumerable mosquitoes added to make the days doubly torturous.

At ten o'clock the door to the cell opened and a ward boy informed me that Professor Sa'ab had come to meet me. I got up and left my cell, walking towards the visitor's area. Just then there was a call from outside the door to the left – 'Behenji, greetings! Praise be to mother India.' Surprised at the sudden sound I looked around but could not make out exactly where it had come from. All I knew was that from somewhere behind the bars separating us, my companions and brothers in struggle were welcoming me in their midst. And at that moment knowing that was enough.

Professorji was sitting in one of the chairs in the office waiting for me. I went and sat down beside him. Looking at me he said, 'There has been a call for a strike in the city. They are trying to get the colleges closed and all over people are picketing and holding demonstrations.' On hearing this, my heart cried out to be with the protestors beyond the walls, but I knew this was no more than wishful thinking.

It did not take long for our twenty minutes together to fly by. A jailor arrived to inform us that the visiting time was over. Standing up immediately, I said namaskar to Professorji and walked back towards my ward.

This time I could see Ward Number 12 in the distance. This was the place where all my companions had been put. I knew they were there but the distance between us was too great for me to make out their faces or recognize them. Voices paying 'Behenji Vande' could be heard. I wished I could stop for a moment and speak to them but I was a prisoner, and being a prisoner I had no rights. With a heavy heart I entered my ward in silence.

Coming into the barrack I sat down on my mat. So many different incidents from the past arose in my memory and danced in front of my eyes. Professorji's words, 'All right, Urmila, goodbye' resounded in my ears. I started thinking. This was only the first day. So far we always used to say that we were slaves, prisoners in our own land, but now, for the first time, I realized what being a slave truly felt like. I couldn't help think of caged birds that wanted so desperately to fly in the sky but could not do so. The thought of birds made me look towards the neem tree that stood in our ward. I could see them perched on the tree and even as I looked on, they spread their wings and flew at will. For a long time I remained caught up in my thoughts. In the afternoon I was given a plate of food that I realized had come from my house. So far I had not had to experience prison food. A slight drizzle began later in the day and I went inside the barrack where the rest of the afternoon was spent in sleep.

It must have been almost 4 p.m. when the ward gates were reopened. From a distance I could see prisoners walking in the prison yard beyond. Chains of iron decorated their limbs. These were the prisoners who had just returned after receiving their verdicts from court. I looked on with interest. Meanwhile, a prisoner carrying a huge iron basin on his head entered our ward. The warden accompanied him. As I soon found out, the basin contained chapattis and the warden was there to distribute food to the female prisoners. 'Come on, take your chapattis,' she called out.

The women moved towards her with their aluminium plates. They were given five chapattis and a bowl of daal each. Wanting to see the kind of food prisoners received, I too went towards the entrance and peeped out. Just then, through the half-opened door I happened to catch a glimpse of Pandit Pyarelal Sharma, Chowdhary Vijaypal Singh, Jagdish Chandra and the other political prisoners of

Meerut as they made their way back to their ward. I cannot explain the happiness and joy that suffused my heart at the sight of these men – it was the way a poverty-stricken man feels when he gets a glimpse of immense wealth. But my joy was short-lived for in a few seconds a servant came and closed the door, bringing an end to my view of what lay beyond.

In the evening, the 'A'-class food arrived for me from the prison. Although it must have been made with special care as compared to the food of the other prisoners, I could not eat it. The flour was full of sand particles that made me flinch with a sense of revulsion each time they came between my teeth. Seeing me leave the food on my plate, the lady warden, in all goodness, told me to eat it and not to fret too much about being in prison. She could not understand that I had put the food away because it was inedible, not because I was sad about being in prison. Knowing that she would not understand what had brought me here, I picked up my plate quietly and distributed the food among the other prisoners.

At six o'clock the door to our ward opened. The jailor entered accompanied by two guards. 'Please go inside,' he said to me. 'It is time to lock up.'

'What! As early as this?' I asked in surprise.

'Yes. As early as this,' came the curt reply.

I went inside. The door of the ward was then closed, a heavy iron chain tied around it and two huge locks secured for the night. The inside door was also locked and we, the three women inside, were locked up till five the next morning.

I could see that the sun was still shining, the sun god spreading his warmth and rosy splendour over the world as the muted rays of evening touched the earth. I started strolling in the little space that the cell afforded. My thoughts drifted to how at this time we would be busy taking out processions in the city. As my imagination took over I could see the procession in front of my eyes – all of us enthused and excited. Men, women, children, the young and the old, marching together with a united call for freedom. Shopkeepers welcomed us to shut down their shops and piles of foreign goods ready to be burnt could be seen everywhere. My skin tingled with the emotion of it all and then suddenly, with a deep sadness I realized that I had been deprived of that life, that now I was no longer a part of it. I came back to earth after that flight of imagination. The sky was still red with the glow of sunset. It was too early to sleep. I lay down. As soon as my head touched the 'bed' the steady drone of mosquitoes announced their intentions for the night, gradually taking over completely. By now even the breeze had stopped. And as the night progressed, the combined onslaught of the mosquitoes and the heat gave me my first taste of what hell was like.

Restlessly I sat and lay and strolled, unable to bear the heat or the insects. Ignoring my discomfort, my two companions started singing a song in their native tongue. It surprised me that even in this hot, sweltering, mosquito-infested night, while I moved from here to there in frustration, they were singing away, happily seated on their mud beds. But the song, though a brave effort no doubt, was born of compulsion. The fact remained that they too were unable to sleep. Somehow midnight passed. I managed to sleep for a short while, only to be woken up by the rude bites of the mosquitoes after which sleep eluded me all night. I hoped dawn was at hand, a matter of only a few more minutes, but the chimes of the prison clock told me it was only two. In an attempt to distract myself, I started chanting all the mantras I knew. Each mantra I had learnt from childhood till now was recalled and recited but even this distraction did not work for too long; the mantras ended, the night did not.

Finally, I think god took pity on me. A cool breeze started blowing and its soothing touch was enough to put me to sleep. But once again the luxury of slumber was short-lived. The front gate clanged and a voice called out: 'Wake up. The door is open.'

3

The Façade of Justice

I woke up to the noise of the front gate clanging. The doors opened, we were counted, and then they were closed again. Having got permission to take a bath, I thanked god for small mercies and stepped outside my barrack.

At around eleven o'clock I was informed that Professorji and some other people had come to meet me. I went to the jailor's office accompanied by a warden and a lady warden, and was completely taken aback to see Pandit Ramswaroop Sharma of the Hindustani Sewa Dal sitting next to my husband. Taken completely by surprise, my face broke into a warm smile at the unexpected sight of my visitor.

'Are you all right?' Professorji asked me. 'Are you having problems here?'

Warmed by his concern, I answered that everything was all right. Reassured, though not entirely convinced by my reply, he shook his head with a knowing smile. I was then informed that my case was to be heard today. Surprised at this piece of information I asked him for the details and we were soon deep in conversation. 'Behenji,' Sharmaji started to say, 'people outside want to see you and…' But before he could complete his sentence or I could respond to the sentiment, my time was up and a guard had arrived to escort me back. Professorji and Sharmaji left the office and I went back to my barrack.

Even though it had been a few days, I was still new to the prison and its ways. To make matters worse I had no companions, just two other women prisoners who remained engrossed in themselves and showed no interest in speaking to me. The constant drone of their voices closed in on me. I went outside my cell and spread my blanket under the neem tree in an attempt to ward off the feeling of claustrophobia. Memories of home, of Professorji, of affectionate conversations with friends, flooded my mind and a surge of emotion overwhelmed me. I shifted restlessly with increasing uneasiness. Finally, in a desperate attempt to erase those images from my mind I closed my eyes and tried to sleep.

Before I knew it I had fallen into a light sleep. Drifting in that stage of semi-consciousness, an image floated behind my closed eyelids – of a huge procession passing through the city. Thousands of people had gathered to walk and protest together. Hundreds of flags waved in the air, adding colour to the march. The procession was being led by a group of women who sang as they moved forward confidently:

Gusts of wind in the garden blew away our home,
We arrived at the gates of prison, searching for a place to belong.
Do not cry, O bird of India,
over memories of the garden now lost to you,,
You were caged for the glory of your song.

Who says it was force by which we were taken?
We came here following our own desire for prison.

The words of the song penetrated deep into my soul and I started singing along with the voices I heard in my head.

You were caged for the glory of your song.

Suddenly the voice of the warden pierced the air. Returning to the present with a jolt, I realized with a sinking feeling that there was no procession here, no voices singing a song. All that remained was my blanket, the prison walls and I.

I went over the words of the song I had been singing. Yes, they were true. After all I *had* come to prison deliberately, consciously, because I *wanted* to. What would have happened if I had not done what I had done, I asked myself. 'It would have been a sin,' my soul replied. 'You have loved your mother. And if *that* is wrong, what in the world could ever be right.' My sense of pride and self-respect joined forces with the voice of my soul. 'If you have ever done anything worthy and honourable in the past twenty-one years of your life, it is this,' it said. I brightened at the realization and was filled with enthusiasm. My spirits restored, I started humming the words I had heard in my head:

Who says we were taken by force?
Our own desire for prison is what has brought us here.

My enthusiasm grew, and I continued singing until I was interrupted by a loud voice.

'It is time,' the sweeper called out. 'Your hearing is about to begin.'

'Good,' I replied happily.

She looked at me in wonder. 'No one knows what the verdict will be.'

'I know, I will be sentenced.'

'For how long?'

'Considering my activities, at least six months.'

The sweeper shook her head, dismayed at the very suggestion. 'Don't say such things, sister,' she said with sympathy.

My hearing was to take place in a small room on top of the main jail entrance. As I stepped out of my barrack I could hear slogans of 'Bharat Mata Ki Jai' raised from the other side of the barred walls. Even without recognizing the people who were calling out, I folded my hands in a gesture of namaskar and moved on.

It was almost three o'clock. A huge crowd had gathered at the main gate. My heart ached to see the large numbers of men, women and children who had collected in the scorching heat to support me. I felt blessed. These were *my* people; they loved me.

From a distance I folded my hands in front of them and walked into the office.

In the room upstairs, Joint Magistrate Mr Kaugil sat at the centre of a large wooden table. A few clerks stood around to assist him. Seats for the public on either side of the table were packed with people. Sharmaji's case had been on before mine, and as soon as it was over I heard my name being called out.

I was given a chair. Seating myself I said, 'Before starting on this case it is important to allow entry to all those people who have already put in their applications to be present here today.' Responding to the validity of the request, many of my political companions and supporters were called up, but due to a shortage of space many of them had to remain standing in the aisles. I also insisted that all the proceedings should take place in Hindi. This too was done.

Finally the hearing began. I was told that I had been accused of inciting students while addressing them at the Town Hall on the thirteenth of the month.

'You had said, "All of you should picket liquor shops and force them to close down. This is your duty." Is this true?'

'Yes, it is true.'

'Your action was illegal and against the law. Because of this a case under the Picketing Ordinance has been registered against you.'

'Very well.'

The proceedings continued. 'Would you like any witnesses to be presented or do you accept the charges?'

'I accept.'

One of my fellow Congress workers later told me that I should not have accepted the charges so easily. 'You should have denied them,' she said. 'At least then we would have been able to see the faces of the traitors who had agreed to testify against you.'

The façade of the proceedings was now over and the magistrate read out his decision.

'You are a leader,' he said, 'and that is why you are being sentenced to only six months in prison. Those who are convicted under this ordinance usually receive a much more severe punishment for their actions.'

I stood up thanking the magistrate for his 'leniency'. Congress workers and supporters covered me with garlands. Returning all their greetings I walked down the stairs. The crowd that had collected there eagerly asked me what the verdict was – 'What happened? What did you get?'

'Six months,' I told them with a smile.

And then, filled with the warmth of my people's blessings, I stepped inside the prison once again. The main gate closed behind me. I knew that as far as I was concerned, it would remain closed for the next six months.

Inside the prison the other political prisoners welcomed me with slogans of freedom and patriotism. I was taken to my barrack and I went inside.

All kinds of thoughts were running through my head. It had not even been a full ten months since my marriage. My father, brothers and sisters were all far away from me in Kashmir. My mother had died four years ago. Soon after that, marriage separated me from my family, and now, even the new life I had started with so many dreams seemed to have been taken away. I realized that for the next 180 days the only friends I would have were the bare stonewalls of prison; my questions would be answered solely by the mute responses of the wind.

Six months. What a long time! But then, suddenly something stirred in my heart. What was I saying? Wasn't this what I had wanted? Even as I collected my thoughts I realized how lucky I was to have had my wish granted. After all, I had come here myself; this was my calling. The mere possibility that my discomfort could in any way lessen the pain of my motherland was enough to wipe out all my apprehensions, all the doubts that had filled my heart earlier.

The other prisoners asked me about my sentence. 'Six months,' I told them with a smile. No trace of the earlier sadness remained. Now there was only a sense of deep joy. I was later told that the other political prisoners who had been arrested along with me were also sentenced to the same term of six months.

4

After the Sentence

The term of my sentence was to begin from the thirtieth of July. Today was just the twentieth. God alone knew when I would be able to go home and be with my friends and family again. I kept imagining the date, dreaming of the moment of my release. With what impatience and enthusiasm would my family await my return that day! They would begin preparations to take me back right from morning, and what immense pleasure they would derive in that! As far as I was concerned, I would get ready the moment I awoke. At exactly ten o'clock they would call me to the jail office where my family would be waiting. The formalities would be completed, I would be released and then I would be allowed to go home. Each time I thought of that day the entire scenario rose before me as if real. With the eyes of my imagination I looked ahead and saw the events as they unfolded – the warden opening the huge iron gate and me walking out of it one step at a time. What happiness, what joy I saw on the faces around me. Again and again they held me, looked at me. Absorbed in that future I closed my eyes. And then, even as a smile curved my lips, a loud noise interrupted my reverie.

Jerking back to reality, I realized that someone was shaking the lock at the door. This was a signal to those inside that the outer door to the barrack had opened and someone was coming in. I had started feeling as if the moment of my release had actually arrived, and I did not want the warmth of the images floating in my mind to be wiped away. I closed my eyes again, wanting to savour each second of that anticipated freedom. The person who entered was the warden. He had come to call me.

'Come on,' he said. 'Get up.' I looked at him in surprise.

'Come on,' he repeated. 'Sahib is calling you. You have to be presented before him.'

I became aware of my surroundings once again. Today was just the first day of my sentence, I realized. Six whole months stretched out in front of me – months I would have to spend here, within these walls, with these companions. I was still trying to come to terms with this fact when the warden came close to me and said in a soft voice, 'Behenji, please come quickly otherwise…'

'Otherwise what?' I asked in alarm.

'Otherwise sahib will want an answer,' he replied ominously.

I got up and followed him out of the door. As soon as I was outside I noticed the prison superintendent, Colonel Abdul Rehman, sitting in a chair in the veranda. In front of him, the prisoners who had already received their sentences stood in two lines. Many of them were satyagrahis, but from a distance it was impossible to recognize them because of the uniformity imposed by the C-Class clothes that all prisoners were made to wear. The prison clerk and doctor stood behind the superintendent in their official uniforms. I was made to stand next to the prisoners lined up.

I could make out that the satyagrahi prisoners wanted to acknowledge my presence in their midst; their eyes reflected the helplessness they felt within their souls. We all knew any attempt to speak would result in a volley of whiplashes. The jailor looked upon them with a cruel glint in his eyes.

Just then the superintendent turned towards me.

'Your name is Urmila Shastri?' he asked.

'Yes.'

'Are you being kept here properly?'

'Yes.'

Looking at me intently he carried on.

'Would you like to put in an appeal against your sentence?'

'No.'

His expression grew grave, but he did not bat an eyelid. Turning towards the sweeper he told her to take me away. The meeting was over.

I came back to the same cell, sat down on the same mat as I had done before. All my earlier sadness seemed to have disappeared. I felt quite pleased with myself. By now the sweeper had started talking to the others. 'See,' she said drawing their attention towards me, 'the superintendent asked her if she wanted to put in an appeal but she refused point blank. Had she gone ahead, she was sure to have been let off.'

Hearing this, one of my fellow women prisoners spoke up with scorn.

'What difference does all this talk of appeal make to her? She can get out whenever she wishes. After all, she has Mahatma Gandhi's hand on her head. He'll get her out whenever she wishes.'

Taken aback at the blatant cynicism of the woman, I asked her, 'But how can he do that? He is in prison himself.'

'Oh, come on,' the woman continued. 'Who has the power to put Gandhiji in prison? I have heard that once they tried to imprison him in seven locks but the next day the locks were found lying on the ground. He had used his powers and come out of the cell.'

'Really? Who told you this story?'

'What's to tell? The entire village knows this is what happened.'

Unable to control my laughter I answered her with a smile. 'You are right. It must have been like that.'

I had no intention of trying to rob these people of the superstitions they had such obvious faith in. But I did feel like sharing their story with someone. Once again the absence of friends struck me with harshness. I realized that I was no longer in a position to share my words, my thoughts or my feelings with the people I wished to. The idea of writing down my feelings crossed my mind but I had no paper. With nothing else to do, I turned to my book and started to read.

Only a few minutes must have passed when I was distracted by the sound of the door being opened again. I looked up and saw a woman enter the barrack. She carried a mat and blanket on her head, an aluminium plate in her right hand and a small child in her left one. The other two prisoners watched her closely. What surprised me most about her was that even though she was as thin as a reed, with cheekbones jutting out of her face and deep wrinkles framing her eyes, there was not a trace of sadness or sorrow in her expression.

The woman seemed to know the warden and wished her. A year earlier she had lived out a one-year sentence in this prison, after which she was transferred to the Fatehgarh Central Jail. Her name was Mohmadi and the warden told me she was a 'Congresswaali'.

Even as we were talking about her, Mohmadi came up to me.

'Salaam bibi,' she said.

'Salaam.'

The lady warden started asking her about the other women prisoners who had been transferred from this jail to the Central Jail in Fatehpur. The conversation continued for a long time. I too was interested in finding out what things were like over there.

'Tell me,' I asked Mohmadi, 'how were you treated when you were there?'

'Oh, don't ask me that, bibi,' she replied. 'They start hitting us at the drop of a hat. The warden in particular was bent on drinking our blood.'

'But I am sure she must have taken care of your pleasure also,' our warden interrupted with a mocking smile.

'Those whom she takes care of are the ones who must be happy. As far as I am concerned I almost ruined my eyes shedding tears because of her.'

Confused at this particular exchange I spoke up on the basis of what I had understood.

'These must be the women who bribe her, isn't it – the ones whom the warden doesn't bother?'

Mohmadi and the warden exchanged a knowing look and smiled. This wordless communication confused me even more.

'What is the matter?' I asked them.

'It has nothing to do with bribing,' I was told. 'What we mean is – the warden there bestows special favours on the girls she finds beautiful.'

The kind of things Mohmadi told me after that made me shudder with revulsion. So shocking were some of her revelations that I cannot even write them here. I do not know how far what I had been told was true, but the mere possibility of its reality was enough to send shivers up my spine.

'Doesn't the lady jailor know about what's going on?' I asked.

'She knows everything.'

'Then why doesn't she do anything? As it is we are all living out our sentences in loneliness, separated from our loved ones. Such treatment on top of that is just inexcusable!' My voice reflected the depth of my feelings about the issue.

Looking at me with a strange mixture of affection and sadness, Mohmadi replied softly, 'Bibi, there is nothing in this world more powerful than bribe.'

Her reply left me silenced. What could I say? She continued.

'There is a huge pit filled with water in our barrack. Sometimes women prisoners push each other's children into this pit when their mothers are not around. Once, a child died because of this. But the warden was fond of the prisoner who had pushed the child in and nothing happened. The incident was hushed up by saying that the child had fallen into the pit by himself.'

For a long time Mohmadi kept me riveted with her stories. I was completely engrossed. It was only when the front gate clanged again and the warden entered to distribute food that I became aware of how much time had passed.

5

A Glimpse of Life in Prison

Until now there had been only two other women in prison and like me they too were here for the first time. But now, with Mohmadi, things changed. She had already spent a year at the Fatehgarh Central Jail and had developed a deep understanding of prisoners and the 'crimes' that brought them to prison. At times it seemed as if she had no regrets whatsoever at leading the life of a prisoner. She had mastered the art of forgetting her sorrows, or at least hiding them beneath an exterior of laughter.

I have always believed that the ability to forget is god's special blessing to mankind. If man were to remain constantly aware of and thinking about his misfortunes, each human being would be perpetually depressed, forever shedding tears of pain, bitterness, sorrow or regret.

Our warden was fond of song and dance and even though she participated in neither of the two, she encouraged it amongst the prisoners. Soon dancing and singing in the female barrack became the norm. I wondered what I had done to deserve being put through the obscenity of such entertainment, something I had never been exposed to in all my life. Unfortunately, the kind of obscenity I am speaking of has not left any section of our society, any district of our country untouched. However, some hope remains – despite its popularity, this vulgar trend has not yet corrupted the songs and dances of our villages. Obscenity, it seems, remains specially, the weakness of urban India.

My father is a committed Arya Samaji. He tries to reflect the principles of his creed in everything he says and does, and has been largely responsible for inculcating them in his children. My mother always assisted him in this. I still remember how as children we were never allowed into the entertainment areas – where singers, dancers and musicians gathered – during weddings. The extent to which this rule was followed can be gauged from the fact that before my marriage I had never seen any play or theatre or musical performance. But this does not mean that I have anything against music. I simply believe that these are arts of the highest sensibilities. They used to occupy a respected and eminent position in ancient India. Music and dance in particular took on unique roles in the form of bhakti sangeet. But the song and dance I witnessed in front of me now was very different from that which was practised in our ancient traditions; it was the kind of spectacle that no decent person would wish to be entertained with. Anyway, this kind of entertainment became the norm in our barrack and with it came the beginnings of hostility and everyday scuffles.

Whatever decency had managed to survive in the face of the obscene onslaught we faced was now made up for in the fights that started breaking out on a regular basis. The lives of the other prisoners (except Mohmadi) were now occupied by vulgarity, abuses and petty altercations.

Very often one of the women would end up crying; that was the note on which most of the fights ended. In any case, whatever their pastimes may have been, at least they were all of the same mentality. I on the other hand had no one; in every sense possible, I was alone in their midst.

One night my patience was stretched to its limit. The main door had been closed for the night when one of the women said, 'Come on, let's make some surma and put it on.' The other woman agreed willingly. Somehow they managed to make some of the concoction with the mustard oil given for their hair. They adorned their eyes with the surma and then, as usual, the fight began. This time the issue was that one of them felt the other had taken too much of the surma for herself and left too little for her, and vice versa. As the two women battled it out amongst themselves I almost went out of my mind. Their screams and yells pierced the air and I itched to make them shut up. If the warden found out they would both be in trouble, but that didn't deter them and they seemed set to tear each other apart. When the cacophony didn't stop till midnight my patience finally gave way and I asked them to keep quiet.

Irritated by my interference, one of them turned to me and said, 'So why don't *you* tell us what exactly I had said.'

The other one followed suit. 'Yes. Go on. Tell us whose mistake it was.'

I kept quiet, determined not to fall into the trap. Faced with my silence they began fighting with each other once again. Finally when I could not take it any longer I called out to the warden. To my complete surprise one of the women also started calling out to warden, heavy sobs accompanying her shouts. She was lucky that the warden didn't hear her or perhaps was not in the mood to take the trouble of opening the iron gates and finding out what was wrong. In either case she did not respond to the yells.

Walking up to the women I tried to explain things to them. 'Look', I said, 'if the warden comes and asks me what is happening I will blame both of you and you will both be in trouble. So let the matter be and just go to sleep. It's very late and we should all try and get some sleep.'

The logic of what I was saying seemed to make sense to the women who quietened down after this. By one o'clock they were both asleep.

But I was not so lucky. Sleep eluded me completely. The thought of spending the remaining months of my sentence with these women made my head reel. At one level I felt that I should not live with them and should move into the other single barrack that had been offered to me. At the same time, I felt that it would be better not to stay alone due to security reasons. In the jail environment where you had no one to protect you, to help you, where even the keys to your door were in other people's hands, it was not sensible to isolate yourself completely. Driven by desperation and need, I folded my hands and prayed to god. 'Dear god,' I said, 'please send some of my companions who have also been arrested into this barrack.' But it seems that my prayer was not driven by the kind of conviction it should have been. God wanted me to put in my share of penance, and so it continued this way for three whole months until I was joined by other political prisoners.

Most of the time I was in prison I had no problem with regard to food. My clothes came from home. A few books and a copy to write in had also been provided. I had asked for sewing material which had been sent from home. In addition to this, the jail authorities started providing a Hindi newspaper to the prisoners twice a week.

For the first week my food was sent from home but then I started cooking. Now the only problem that remained was that of loneliness. I had drawn up a rough routine to combat this enemy and I stuck to it meticulously. Hours turned to days, days to weeks, and second by second, my time in prison gradually passed.

In time I got accustomed to this new life I was leading away from the familiarity of the outside world. After speaking to the jailor it had been agreed that the front gates would now be closed only at night. It was now possible to sit and stroll in the prison yard till late evening, something that I really enjoyed. The days were very hot and because of the constant strain my eyes were under, they would start smarting by evening. I had also developed a constant nagging headache by this time. Word of my ill-health was sent to the superintendent and one day, early in the morning, I was called to his office.

Accompanied by the lady warden I went there to find Mr Rehman, the superintendent, sitting at his table.

'Is it true that you are having trouble with your eyes?' he asked me.

'Yes.'

'What is the matter with them?'

I explained the problem to him in detail.

After listening to me carefully he said, 'All right. We will get your eyes examined either tomorrow or day after. It is possible that you may need to use spectacles.'

But this did not satisfy me. 'I would like to consult a specialist,' I spoke up. 'Please send for Captain Tandon. He is an eye specialist.'

'Why Doctor Tandon in particular?' the superintendent asked me coldly. 'Are you interested in getting your eyes checked or in the doctor?'

'I just mean a specialist, someone who is reliable in his diagnosis.'

'And who do you propose will pay the fees for a specialist?'

'I am in jail,' I said assertively, 'and all my medical treatment should be carried out as per the rules and regulations of the prison.' Rehman was losing his patience by now. 'The prison is not responsible for the eyes and teeth of its prisoners.'

'All right. If my request cannot be fulfilled, let it be. I'll get my eyes checked later.'

Rehman frowned. 'When?'

'Six months later when I am out of prison,' I said firmly.

'All right,' he answered. 'You can go back now.'

Without saying a word I returned to my ward. Even though I did not show it, in my heart of hearts I was quite worried about what would happen if my eyes continued to deteriorate. I knew that I needed medical attention, but I was also aware that the jail authorities were supposed to show me to a good doctor and I was not willing to compromise on my rights. But to my very pleasant surprise, a few days later Superintendent Rehman arrived with a European eye specialist and got my eyes checked. The required medicines were also provided after that.

The next day the collector was supposed to come on a round of the prison. By now I had understood that each time a senior official came on a round, all attempts were made to fulfil the requests of the prisoners.

Early the next morning the main ward was opened and prisoners were given the permission to carry out a special cleaning of their cells. Lines were prepared for the parade. At exactly 9 a.m. the collector entered the ward accompanied by the superintendent. Without paying any attention to the other prisoners he approached me. I stood up. The collector came up to me and asked, 'Are you all right here?'

'Yes, I am.'

'Are there any problems that you are facing?'

'None, thank you.'

'Tell me, what were you doing just now?'

I showed him my pillow which I had been sewing before he entered. The sight seemed to reassure him that all was well.

'All right then,' he said. 'Have a good day.'

I went inside and the collector left without asking the other two women prisoners anything. As he passed them the superintendent gave one of them a withering, scornful look. I knew that with the end of the official's visit the examination of the jail authorities was also over and they knew that they had passed the test.

Even more important than the collector's visit was the day when the inspector general of police, the highest ranking jail officer of the district, visited the jail. The walls were whitewashed and the entire building went through a thorough cleaning. For two days before the visit no employee of the prison had a spare moment. Finally, on the twenty-sixth of August the inspector general arrived. As per routine I was presented before him when he visited the female ward. Starting off with the usual questions he asked,

'Are you all right here? Is there anything you need?'

'I am well, thank you,' I replied. 'But if you could provide me with a charkha I will appreciate it greatly. That way I can spin my wheel and pass my time more easily.'

Shaking his head the inspector general replied that the charkha could not be provided to any prisoner.

'But as far as I have heard, A-Class prisoners are provided with charkhas in other prisons,' I insisted.

'We will find out,' said the inspector general and then ending the topic moved on to more general enquiries. 'Other than that is there anything else you require?'

'Yes,' I replied. 'I am very lonely here. I get to meet visitors only once in every fifteen days. I would like it if instead of the permission to write letters I be allowed to meet visitors twice instead of once in this time span.'

To this also the inspector general had a ready response. 'We will send you to the Lucknow prison,' he said. 'There are lots of other female political prisoners like yourself over there.' Ending the conversation, he left the ward, discussing my case with the superintendent.

It was only after he had left that the implications of his offer struck me. What if they actually sent me to Lucknow? There was no doubt that the almost solitary confinement in this prison was a source of great depression for me and had even started manifesting itself in my health. Even Professorji had mentioned many times that it would be much better if I got transferred to Lucknow. But the thought of leaving Meerut filled my heart with sadness. There was something about the city that I felt connected to, and the mere prospect of being away from it filled me with emptiness. A new chapter of my life had started in Meerut. Leaving my parental home in Kashmir, this was the city where I had made my own home, laid the foundations of a new beginning for myself. Despite being in prison I still felt as if I was close to home. And that was the reason why I didn't want to go away from here despite all the conveniences the other alternative may have offered me.

The next time Professorji came to visit me I was reassured on being told that the inspector general had changed his mind about sending me to Lucknow. I also asked if any progress had been made with regard to the charkha. To my horror, Professorji told me that instead of allowing me to have a charkha, the inspector general had sent a circular to all the prisons instructing them to take away any charkha that any of political prisoner might have. I was filled with guilt and cursed myself for having brought the issue up with the authorities. A feeling of great sadness settled on me as I realized that so many of my companions had been deprived of their charkhas because of me.

The request to replace my letter-writing privilege with another visiting day was valid even as per the directives of the jail manual. Professorji had written about this in the newspapers and to the inspector general as well. Finally, the latter sent for the order and interpreted it to be applicable only to C-Class prisoners and not to either class A or class B ones. I knew that even C-class political prisoners were not allowed to take advantage of this provision. In the end I consoled myself by saying that I had been sent to prison to suffer hardship and my loneliness was after all just another part of that hardship; all these were sufferings that I would gladly bear for the sake of my motherland.

During all this time other satyagrahi leaders remained very worried about me. I heard that Pandit Pyarelal Sharma, Quazi Nizammuddin and Maulana Abul Kalam Azad in particular tried very hard to get me permission to meet some of my political companions who were also in prison, but permission was always denied. For three months – until I was joined by my satyagrahi sisters – I continued to live in isolation. That was the time I realized that we are social creatures – that our need for companionship and human interaction is as important if not as basic as our need for air and food and water.

However, no matter how difficult those months of solitude may have been, in retrospect I realize that without them I would never have been able to streamline and intensify my thought process in the way that my role as a leader required me to do. In that sense, my solitude was well compensated.

By and large there were only three of us in the barrack, but there was a time when for a few days around fifteen other women, all of them under-trials, also occupied the barrack. As was expected, frequent fights between these women became the order of the day and the warden started organizing daily parades to counter this tendency. Sometimes when hostilities ran low, the women would sit together and exchange the stories of their lives. With tears running down their faces, each one of them would narrate her personal tragedy. At times like this even I got drawn into what they had to say.

On one such occasion, seeing my attention drawn towards them, the women started speaking amongst themselves.

'Doesn't she regret coming to jail like this?' one of them asked gesturing towards me.

Her companion was quick to respond. 'Of course she must be regretting it. She must have got carried away in the heat of the moment with all the patriotic fervour and courted arrest, and now there's nothing she can do about it.'

'Yes, that must be it. Otherwise why would she remain so reserved and withdrawn. Never even talks to anyone.'

With these words she gave me a warm look and her friend started talking to me.

'Sister, why did you get involved in all these politics?' she said. 'You should have let the men handle it. It is the way of the world to stand back and enjoy other people's troubles. See, you have been here for so long and no other companion of yours has come to join you.'

Hearing these words I smiled to myself. What could I say to these women? I thought. How could I make them understand?

At around nine o'clock each night the sweeper would enter the barrack accompanied by a man who distributed chapattis, and each day without fail, a share of the prisoner's chapattis ended up in the stomach of the lady warden. Those women who refused to part with their food incurred her wrath and had to face her ire sooner or later. After dinner the main ward would be closed and once again it would be time for gossip, squabbles and arguments.

Sometimes the monotony of the routine was broken by a storytelling session. One night the topic chosen was that of ghost stories. One of the women said, 'The sweeper was telling me that there is a grave of a sufi saint in this ward and the ghost of that saint can be see walking around on Mondays and Fridays.'

'Yes,' joined in another woman. 'He is always accompanied by a cat. If it is twelve o'clock on a Friday night and you look towards the grave, you can even see him saying his prayers. The cat keeps strolling around. If you make a wish when you see it, it is sure to be granted.'

'But how can that be?' I asked in amazement.

'It's true,' she replied confidently. 'I can even show it to you. You can ask the sweeper if you don't believe me.' By now it was quite late and the matter got put off till the next day. When the sweeper arrived next morning, I asked her about the story.

'Is it true that the ghost of the sufi saint can be seen here?' I asked her.

'Oh yes,' she replied. 'I have seen him. One of the prisoners who had committed a murder also saw it once and became a believer after that. She made it a point to pour milk on the grave every day, and the pir blessed her in such a way that despite a clear case against her she was let off without any punishment.'

The matter finished here. Then one Friday night, I was startled out of my sleep by a frantic sound. One of the prisoners was calling out my name.

'Bibi, bibi,' she called out in fright.

'Yes, what is it?' I asked still half-asleep.

'Pirji's cat is walking near your head.'

I jerked out of my sleep. Turning around I saw a fat black cat sitting near my pillow. The cat looked straight at me and then walked away. The other prisoner who had been watching me said in a soft voice, 'The saint is pleased with you, bibi. You can wish for anything you want.'

I did not say anything and seeing my lack of response, she started praying.

'O great power, messenger of the god above,' she said, 'please grant that my fellow prisoners are released from the cruel and unjust clutches of the prison authorities.'

She went on for a while and after her prayer was finally over she said her namaaz. All this while, I had said nothing. I just watched her in silence and gradually the entire thing lost the eeriness it had contained before. As I lay down to sleep again, my last thoughts were about the unnecessary fuss made over a mere cat.

As the days passed, I came to the conclusion that no culprit, no matter how severe a crime he or she might have committed, should be sent to the prisons of India. At times I thought about what the best way to rehabilitate these prisoners could be. I felt that a workshop should be organized where learned people should be called to come and talk to these people, teach them and guide them. Sitting alone in my cell I would often find myself imagining these workshops. It used to be a wonderful pastime. I thought of a huge hall, just like the prison, but clean and beautiful. It was divided into different sections where the prisoners were taught different skills; all of them were dressed in clean clothes, not the tattered filthy ones they now wore. Such were the dreams I would lose myself in until the cruel reality that we were all prisoners, all slaves, reasserted itself. And then, all my beautiful imaginings, the proud creations of my mind would shatter and fall to the ground like dust.

6

Divine Ambrosia

By now each barrack of the prison was filled with political prisoners who had courted arrest. Each dawn was accompanied by the strains of some nationalistic song or the other. The fragrant breeze that blew through the corridors of prison carried the notes of the melody to each person present there, reinforcing the enthusiasm and pride already existing in our hearts. All of us in the barracks would then pledge allegiance to our motherland and our flag, in silence yet again. I still don't know where my sadness disappeared on hearing the notes of those songs each morning. It was as if the life-giving ambrosia of those songs was sent to us by god himself. They went on and on. Even as I lay in the restricted and oppressive boundaries of the female ward, the notes of those songs drifted in – indistinct yet ever so soothing – through all the walls and locks and chains that separated me from my revolutionary companions outside.

As I went over the words of the songs I would get transported to the green open fields of my country, fields where I felt even the gods were engrossed in the worship of my native land. Gathering all my senses I concentrated on the drifting sounds so as not to miss out on a single word:

May our beloved tricolour remain ever-high,
Ever-fluttering in the wind,
The conqueror of this entire universe.
Forever showering strength,
Forever teaching the healing of love,
The one to inspire and enthuse our heroes,
The soul of our land.
Let its pride be never diminished
Even if lives are lost to that end.
Only when the universe has been conquered
Will our pledge be fulfilled.

Fearless under the proud banner of this flag,
Unshakeable, we take the pledge of freedom,
Raising the slogan of praise to our motherland,
Freedom our ultimate goal.
Beloved, this land of ours.
Victory, Victory.

Come O brave warriors come,
Sacrifice yourselves for the sake of your land
Come and sing together one and all.

This song seemed filled with some strange power. As I hummed it, my soul filled with heady, intoxicating happiness. Whenever my heart was restless and the traumas of prison life became intolerable, this song – this sweet strength-giving ambrosia would restore and sustain me. Sitting in the barrack, whenever I heard it, immediately, even without wishing it myself, I would be suffused with passion and patriotism. Some unarticulated desire would make me strong, powerful and unafraid. Each inch of my being would want to sing along with the others in the barracks outside, but I could not do so. I was all alone here, and without any companion such action would be futile. Days passed by and I could not figure out how to transform this wish of mine into action, into fulfilment.

The song was sung twice each day, morning and evening. Before the notes from one ward could be silenced, the prisoners of the other ward would start. As the crescendo rose, the entire prison reverberated with the words and the images of that one song:

May our flag remain forever high!

And finally, once it was over, the finale would resound, combining in itself all the peace and strength that our struggle had come to signify:

Praise be to our Motherland!
Praise be to Mother India!
Praise be to our beloved Tricolour!

The words echoed gloriously all around. And hearing the echoes of an entire nation reflected in the powerful voices, the authoritarian and dictatorial regime of colonialism shuddered in its offices and homes.

For me, if there was any positive aspect to my stay in prison, it was this. Not a single day passed when some patriot, driven by love for his motherland and devoured by his hunger for freedom and liberty, did not come to join the ranks of his imprisoned brothers.

This song marked arrivals as well as departures. From eleven to two each afternoon the departures were celebrated and in the evenings all the new arrivals welcomed with equal fervour. Before my companions arrived, this song was the only consolation of my prison life. And gradually, even our ward started getting affected by the meanings and promises that resounded in the walls of the prison. A perceptible change seemed to be coming over the prisoners of my barrack, who, till now indifferent and uninvolved, could not help be moved by its power.

7

Tears of Blood

How can I ever forget those days of my life when I witnessed the children of doting mothers being flayed by whips and canes. Those pages are written in my memory with the indelible ink of human blood. The young, innocent bodies of those men were ignorant of violence. They had been imprisoned and punished not because of any crime they committed but because of their love for their motherland. Even today my heart shudders to recall those horrifying moments. Sometimes I can still feel as if young Shanti Sharan is being beaten in front of me. His only crime: going on a nineteen-day hunger strike. I can still hear his screams resounding in my ears. It was eight o'clock in the morning on the twenty-ninth of August. The superintendent was checking on the prisoners as they filed past his table. Just then a sweeper, Ashraf Ali, presented the names of a few prisoners to him.

'What is the matter?' the superintendent asked. After being told whatever the matter was, he asked the named men to be presented in front of him.

'Sahib,' the sweeper said, 'they do not let us complete the counting at night and create a lot of trouble.'

After he finished speaking, sounds of complete commotion suddenly filled the prison. Shouts rose in the air accompanied by the slogans of 'Praise be to Mother India'. I sat up in my bed. What was this new thing happening in the prison today? I went and stood at the gate but nothing was visible. Suddenly the alarm bell of the prison started ringing. The authorities started pushing all the prisoners into the barracks, stuffing them inside forcefully, and gradually the commotion seemed to settle down. And then, like a bolt out of the blue, loud screams were heard from one of the barracks. Along with the screams we could also hear the relentless swishing of a cane.

'The political prisoners are being beaten with canes!' someone from the cell whispered. Under the blistering heat of the afternoon sun, the cruel soldiers had stripped the prisoners in the yard and were raining heartless blows on their defenceless bodies. Streams of blood started flowing. Small chunks of flesh fell off the bodies. Even then the doctor did not raise his hand to bring an end to the torture. The canes broke. The superintendent then gave orders for a new set of canes to be bought so that the beating could be continued. This was the naked face of cruelty and barbarism, the dark image of human heartlessness.

Such was the extent of the prisoner's agony that pain herself was moved to comfort them. Taking them into her wings she embraced them, and one by one all the prisoners crossed over from the threshold of pain into unconsciousness. Even the birds, it seemed, were unable to endure the sight and had flown away from their usual perches on the prison trees. Still the relentless sound of the cane continued. I ran and stood near the bars of my prison ward even though my hands did not have the strength to break them. Anger, guilt and compassion combined in a single heart-wrenching emotion that shook my entire being. But I was helpless, what could I do. 'O god!' I screamed out.

'Where are you?' It was in that moment that I realized what people mean when they speak of 'tears of blood'.

The next prisoner in line for the treatment was the brave revolutionary Mukhtar Singh. The warden made him take off his clothes. Looking at him, Sahib said, 'Oh, so this is the same Mukhtar Singh!'

'Yes sir,' the line inspector responded, 'the same Mukhtar Singh who gave up his job with the police to join the Congress.' Our companion was tied to the pillar in the middle of the yard. Even after thirty lashes he remained conscious, sustained and soothed by the constant chanting of his nation's name. Not once, not even for a second, did that name leave his lips.

Once the official beating was over, the bodies of the prisoners were flung like corpses in a cell. Just then the door opened for the afternoon meal. The half-dead men made a request to meet me, their sister in struggle. In response, the door was opened slightly, just enough for me to be able to peep outside. When I looked out I saw all of them covered in blood – thirteen brave freedom fighters lying on the burning ground, drifting between consciousness and unconsciousness, drenched in sweat and blood. Shanti Sharan was still in chains and even in that condition I saw him fold his hands and greet me. 'Behenji, today your companions have been treated very cruelly.'

I had no words with which to respond. What could I have said to him at that point? Finally, in an attempt to console and encourage them, I said, 'I have full faith in god. He will ensure justice for this outrage. The spilt blood of innocent men never goes waste. It always extracts its price.'

Later Ashraf Ali told me the entire story.

'It was quite late at night,' he began. 'We had gone to do the daily counting but these men did not let us. Next morning, when it was time to present them before the magistrate, they started running all around in the barrack and refused to come out. It was only when they started breaking the doors that sahib got the prison alarm rung. That is why the collector sahib insisted on punishing them himself. Eighty rods from the main gate have been broken. All the solitary confinement cells have been damaged.'

I was unconvinced. 'What was the real story?' I wondered. In time I got to know the truth.

Each evening the counting of heads was done when the prisoners lined up outside their barracks for the evening prayers. After this they were sent inside. But that day the prisoners were sent inside without being counted. At around eight o'clock the warden arrived at the barrack and asked the men to line up outside so that the counting could be done. The men, exhausted by the day's exertions, requested him to come inside and complete the job. The warden did not agree. Neither did the prisoners.

At this point the policemen accompanying the warden tried to get the men out forcibly. They were kicked, pulled and dragged. When even this did not work, the warden counted them and then, noting down the names of a few of them, left. After this incident all the prisoners were convinced that the next day they would be chained and sent to solitary confinement. Next morning, when a few selected satyagrahis were called out for being presented before the magistrate, all of them insisted on being taken there together. Demanding this, they came out of the barrack and stood outside together. The wardens tried to push them back into the barracks. When all attempts to get the prisoners inside failed, they tried to divide the group by bribing some of the prisoners with offers of an early release, in return for help in getting their companions inside. Far from working, the ruse had the opposite effect and prisoners from other barracks, who had been inside so far, also started coming out in support of their companions. Seeing the confusion, a number of convicts decided to take advantage of the situation. They too joined the political prisoners and while everyone was distracted, they tried to break open the main gate and escape unnoticed. Later it was said that the satyagrahis had broken eighty rods of the main gate. While this was a gross exaggeration, it was nonetheless true that a few rods had been broken. However, it would have been impossible in that chaos for the authorities to make out whether it was the political prisoners who were damaging the building or the others. The problem was compounded by the fact that all the prisoners – political and criminal alike – used to be kept together and wore the same prison uniforms.

The possibility that Shanti Sharanji in particular, who had been kept in solitary confinement and without food for the past nineteen days, or sixteen-year-old Banerjee who weighed hardly anything, could have been responsible for breaking the solid rods of the prison gate seemed quite ridiculous to me. How thirteen prisoners, all of them political, were identified for the act and how it was decided that they be caned so mercilessly remains a mystery to me. The collector on the other hand, I am sure, is aware of the answer.

At this stage I would like to mention that when the above-mentioned punishment was being meted out to the thirteen satyagrahis in question, the collector of Meerut, Mr Pedley, the inspector general of prisons and the joint magistrate, Mr Cogill, were all present in the prison. It was in the presence of all of them that this gross abuse of justice was ordered and carried out.

According to the rules laid down in the Jail Manual, before a prisoner can be flogged, caned, or whipped, he first had to be medically examined to ensure that he is physically strong enough to endure the punishment. As I have already mentioned, Shanti Sharan had been fasting for nineteen days. He had broken his fast only the previous day and it can be well imagined just how prepared he would have been to endure such brutality. Nevertheless, the medical officer had just stood by and watched as the prisoners were caned. He had not said a word. The prisoners – Shanti Sharan, Manohar Lal, Mukund Lal, Meghraj, Bihari Lal, Lal Singh, Harvansh, Mukhtar Singh, Rajkumar, Bhagirath, Shitabh Rai, Surajbhaan and B.N. Banerjee – were caned thirty times each.

This incident created an atmosphere of terror in the prison for days to come. Every attempt was made to ensure that no news could leak out from the prison, as the authorities did not want anyone to know about the unforgivable atrocity they had committed on political prisoners in their custody.

As would be understandable, after this incident I became much more impatient to meet Professorji. Finally the day arrived. As any prisoner knows, the day one gets to meet one's family has a sanctity no less than that a moment of worship. Although the visiting hours were between 3 p.m. and 4 p.m. we started preparing for them since morning. Different thoughts filled my mind: 'I wonder who will come today? I must remember to ask for such and such thing. I must remember to ask about this matter.' As it is, the hours of waiting stretched on forever but today they seemed to be even longer. It was almost 5 p.m. and no one had come to inform me of any visitors. As the minutes ticked away, my heart sank in depression followed by a sense of apprehension. 'What could have happened?' I wondered. 'What if Professorji is not well?' Unable to rein in my thoughts I started walking up and down the barrack. Just then the door opened. My heart skipped a beat. I was sure the call would be for me. Not wanting to appear too eager I came into my cell and opened a book, pretending to read. But when no one called for me for a few seconds I looked up to find that it was just the usual distribution of the evening tea that was taking place outside.

The warden came up to me and asked me to take my tea. With great difficulty I kept my voice from wavering and told her that I would not have tea as yet.

'Why?'

'Today is my visitor's day. Why haven't I been called as yet?'

'Today you won't have any visitors.'

'Why?' I asked in shock, unable to believe my ears.

The warden shrugged her shoulders. 'I don't know,' she said.

'I have a right to be told the reason for this denial of my rights.'

Looking uncomfortable, she came closer and whispered, 'Please don't tell anyone I told you this, but sahib has ordered your visiting rights to be stopped.'

'All right then,' I said. 'Go and tell him that until I am given the reason for not being allowed to meet my visitors I will not eat anything.'

The warden left.

For a moment I felt as if my head was swimming. I sat down. Both the jailor and the superintendent had not visited my cell for the last few days and I could think of no reason behind this sudden denial of my rights.

Before I could think of anything else, the door opened again. This time the prison clerk entered the barrack along with the same food bearer as before. Coming straight to my cell he said, 'Please eat some food.'

'Before that I want an answer to my question.'

'Jailor sa'ab says that no one came to meet you today.'

'You are mistaken. I have reason to believe that the jail authorities have withdrawn my visiting rights. I wish to know why and on what grounds this was done.' I received no answer and like the warden before him, the clerk also returned without any success. I resigned myself to receiving neither an answer nor any food and to present myself before the superintendent. A little while later the assistant warden entered with some food and started persuading me to eat it. But even he had no answer to my question and kept repeating the same story that I had had no visitors. Finally, losing my temper at last, I turned towards him and said firmly, 'Jailor sa'ab, none of you need to come and meet me until you have the answer to my question. I will not eat.'

It was nine o'clock at night. The barrack had been locked. I came inside and was lying in my cell when the front gate opened once again. It was the same clerk who had visited me earlier. Walking up to my cell he said, 'Sahib has cancelled your visiting rights for the next three days. And not just yours but also those of all class A and B political prisoners. Those implicated in the Meerut conspiracy case are also facing the same cancellation. Now that you have received the answer to your question, I assume you have no more complaints to make. Please eat your food now.'

With these words he left, closing the main gate behind him. I noticed that although he had reminded me to eat, he had very conveniently forgotten to give me my share of food.

A few days later I happened to meet the assistant jailor again. Sitting in front of him I was talking to the visitors who had come to meet me. In the course of the conversation, Professorji asked me whether or not I was getting any ice.

'No,' I replied. 'I think it may be because of the way in which the Meerut conspiracy case is proceeding. I've been told that the contractor brings a very limited amount each day.'

Hearing this, the jailor spoke up at once. 'Mrs Shastri, you cannot carry on with this conversation. This amounts to complaining against and criticizing the jail authorities. It is not permitted.'

I stopped myself from making a reply and we began talking of other things. 'My eyes seem to have become really weak,' I continued. 'I am not even able to read and write as often and as much as I would like to.'

'But how did that happen?' Professorji asked with concern.

'I don't know. Perhaps it is because of excessive exposure to the sunlight. Usually I remain in the barracks but the day the political prisoners were caned I was also standing in the sun from twelve to two in the afternoon. Maybe that is one of the things that aggravated it.'

As usual Professorji was full of questions. 'Did you see Shanti Sharan that day?' he asked. 'It is believed that he was in a very bad condition.' Once again the jailor interrupted. 'You cannot talk about this matter. It is prohibited.'

'Then please tell us what we can talk about,' my husband answered in irritation. 'At every sentence you tell us we are not allowed to speak on such and such topic. Please write down all the disallowed topics on a piece of paper. I will go to Mr Pedler, the collector, myself, and ask him what things I can and cannot speak to my wife about.'

Undeterred, the jailor continued. 'All political conversations are prohibited,' he said. 'Other that that, you can talk about whatever you wish.'

But Professorji was not one to be intimidated. He looked at the jailor with equal confidence. 'I have read the Jail Manual very well and at no point is there any clause stating that political issues and conversations are not to be allowed.'

'I don't know about the Jail Manual but I do know that you cannot carry on such conversations here.'

Until then there had been no such prohibitory provision in the Jail Manual, but within a few weeks the government passed orders and a new clause to that effect was included. One of my biggest regrets was that twenty precious minutes of my visiting time were wasted in this unproductive argument that day.

The next day I was visited by the superintendent. Walking straight up to me he said in a stern voice, 'Hello Mrs Shastri. Please tell your visitors not to bring up any political issues with you when they are and not to try and instigate trouble. Otherwise your visiting rights will be suspended.' The statement was made in such a rude and offensive manner that even I lost my temper.

'Who has been reporting my conversations to you?' I asked.

'Jwala Prasad, the assistant jailor.'

'He is lying,' I responded in anger.

'I do not want any trouble, Mrs Shastri.'

'What you want or do not want is not my concern. And you are most welcome to terminate my visiting rights if you want. I can handle that. If fact, you can go ahead and inflict whatever atrocities you wish, violate any rights. I will bear all of it without complaint.'

Then pausing for a second I continued, 'When you are fully aware that I never break any rules of the prison how can you come and accuse me of such things on the basis of a one-sided accusation?'

Seeing my response the superintendent seemed to realize that the import of his words might go beyond the walls of the prison and have repercussions within the public. The jailor also whispered something into his ear. Turning to me again he spoke in a softer and less aggressive voice.

'So you tell me, what was the conversation that had occurred?'

I related the basic gist of the conversation to him. He did not say anything. But just before exiting the cell he turned back and said, 'Why did Shanti Saran's name come up? That was unnecessary.'

Until this particular incident I had never been told about what I should or should not talk about during my visiting hours. However, that day the point had been made, the rules laid down. It was enough to make me realize that things had indeed changed.

8

Treatment of Prisoners

The Indian police force has the reputation of being the most corrupt in the world. In direct contrast to the functions of public assistance and protection that it has in other countries, in India the force seems to exist with the sole purpose of harassing and exploiting its people. In the smaller villages of the country, the mere mention of the police, even today, is enough to scare and intimidate people. The situation in the prisons of the country is even more depressing. As it is, rules and regulations of the prison system are extremely rigorous, and they are made to bear down hard on the inmates. Yet it is my experience that despite the rigid hardness of the system, the overall environment – good or bad – depends almost entirely on the personal disposition – good or bad – of the officer in charge.

As a rule, kind-hearted men are not put in charge of prisons. Even if they are, the system and its functional coldness, bordering almost on inhumanity, soon corrupt them. I'm sure there must be very few superintendents and jailors who investigate any problem within their prisons properly. The word of the wardens is taken without giving any thought to hearing both sides of the story. And even in the rare cases where other prisoners do give their evidence, they always say whatever the warden threatens them to. If they do not do this, the warden gets even with them at the first opportunity available. At the slightest excuse prisoners are warned of solitary confinement, beatings and chains. So great is the fear they inspire that prisoners always have to be careful to remain in their good books. In addition to all this, they also extract money from the prisoners whenever possible; money that I'm sure amounts to much more than what their salaries are.

I remember, a few days before my release, a new lady warden arrived. One day she came to our ward in connection with some visitors who had arrived to meet a C-Class prisoner. The 'visitors' were the woman prisoner's young daughter and her four-year-old son. As soon as the son saw his mother he started crying loudly. On the other side of the prison bars the mother also started crying. All who were witness to the scene felt their eyes grow moist at the raw emotion on display, but the cruel, hard-hearted warden was not moved. Standing between the children and their mother she refused to move until she was given some money.

The daughter looked at her with pleading eyes. 'I have only four annas,' she said. 'And I have to back to my village. If I give this money to you how will I pay the ikkewalla.' But the warden was not interested in any reason. 'Nothing doing,' she snapped. 'Wanting to meet her mother and doesn't even have the money to pay for it. What do you think? These prison meetings come for free? Stupid girl!'

The mother folded her hands and begged the warden again. 'Please let us meet. As it is we have lost so much time. Just allow us a few minutes with each other.' But her pleas fell on deaf ears. The girl then took out four paise and put them on the table in front of her.

Yet the warden was not satisfied. 'What is this?' she asked scornfully. 'Do you think I'll let you meet for just four paise? Is that why I got you till here?'

The girl looked at her mother in desperation. Finally the woman said, 'Let it be, beti. Give her all the money. You can beg on the way back but after this we will not have a chance to meet for another three months.' The girl did as her mother said and took out all the money she had, putting it on the table. The warden looked around carefully and then took off her shoe. 'Put it in here,' she said. 'Carefully. Make sure no one sees you.'

Seeing this, the mother started crying bitterly. Her helplessness shook my entire being. 'O god! Is it not enough that today my children will have to travel home on an empty stomach that you are putting them in a situation where they will have to beg as well?' she cried in anguish. 'All my life I will have to live with the thought that despite my being alive, my children had to beg.'

Anyone who witnessed the scene between that mother and her children would have been moved by its pathos, but it seems that the people in charge of prisons have neither the heart nor the humanity to enable them to feel the pain of others.

Although cruelty and injustice were the norm in prison, their worst impact was on the poor, illiterate people who were not even aware of their rights. There were rules and regulations for everything in prison – how to parade, how to put forward your requests to the officer concerned, how to live properly, how to spend your time etcetera. Anyone can see how important it is to make sure that prisoners are aware of these rules, but no attention was paid to this. I often saw large numbers of prisoners being presented to the superintendent for breaking rules and then being punished for their lapses. At the time these punishments were meted out the prisoners were never asked anything. Did anyone ever bother to find out if they were even aware of what they were supposed to do and not do? Of whether they even realized and understood what they were being punished for?

To give an example, whenever a prisoner wanted to ask the superintendent anything he was supposed to raise his hand once the parade was over. Only when he was asked to speak was he supposed to do so. Those of us who were educated could see the pattern and figure out the rules even if we were not told about them. But the prisoners of the C class were usually villagers who could not understand this system and would often speak up out of turn. They could not be held responsible for this breach of code as no one had bothered to explain the rules to them to being with. Yet they would be punished. The poor people kept suffering the injustice inflicted on them. They must have been crying out in the silence of their hearts; that was all they could have done.

The jail superintendent, Colonel Rehman, was concerned with nothing other than bossing around and asserting his control over others. He would enter the wards with aplomb, his arrival announced by the barking of his dogs. The dogs accompanied him everywhere even though getting them within the premises was against the rules of the prison. After that, with the jailor, the doctor and a member of the CID in tow, he would make his grand entry into the ward, followed by an attendant who meticulously fanned his back, making sure no fly sat on it. Behind the attendant would be two policemen and the warden. Perhaps he felt less threatened when he entered our particular ward and the two policemen remained outside, near the door.

For some strange reason, the superintendent sahib, despite being Indian, liked to give people the impression that he did not speak Hindustani, and hence made it a point to speak to everyone only in English. I asked him to speak to me in Hindustani many times, but he seemed to find it very difficult to comply with my request. Every second minute he had to take the help of the jailor to provide him with the required words in 'our' language. Had he been British the matter would have been different, but here was this 'gentleman', an Indian by birth and blood, yet so uncomfortable with the language of his own country. Maybe even a British officer would have managed to speak broken Hindustani when required, but this particular brown 'sahib' was too ashamed to utter even a word that was not in English. This is perhaps the dilemma that we as a people are destined to live with – this obsession with all things foreign is the shameful image of our slavery, of the psychological servitude that has invaded our minds!

When superintendent sahib could not speak in Hindustani even to me, I can well imagine what conversations he must have had with the poor C-class prisoners who were completely uneducated. But yes, being rude and insulting seemed to be his forte. Since he never made any concessions even for me – the only female political prisoner there – I can imagine how obnoxious his behaviour with the prisoners in the male ward must have been.

As long as Superintendent Rehman remained in charge of the prison I maintained one complaint against him – he never explained the rules of the prison to anyone nor did he follow them himself. Till the very end he did not have a fixed time to visit the women's ward. And why would he? After all, didn't he consider himself to be the lord and master of the jail?

Many times the warden would announce his arrival just as I had gone for a bath and I would have to rush out to present myself, putting on my clothes again without having bathed. I hoped that he would inform us of his arrival at least half an hour before his visit, but to no avail. In contrast, I have to say without any hesitation that when a British officer, Major Clyde, succeeded Superintendent Rehman, this complaint of mine was done away with forever.

It is with a sense of great shame that I have to admit that while the behaviour of the Indian superintendent with the female prisoners was always arrogant and irreverent, that of his British counterparts was above reproach. The manner in which they made it a point to respect the dignity of the women in the prison was truly commendable. During the time I spent in prison, I had the opportunity to come in contact with two British superintendents. The first was a Major Yule, who had come as a replacement for Superintendent Rehman while the latter was on leave for a week, and the other was Major Clyde, who succeeded him. The behaviour of both these officers towards me was always courteous and decent. How different this was from the way our own Indian officers treated us! Whenever I think about this, my heart grows cold and I cannot stop myself from thinking what kind of leaders my fellow Indians will make when the time comes. Earlier, I had often heard of comparisons being made between Indian and British officers, but now I experienced that difference myself. How far have my Indian brothers fallen, how greatly have they strayed under the rule of the conquerors. But then, all this was no surprise; it is in keeping with the very mechanisms of colonialism and imperialism.

Mahatma Gandhi was right. He always said that the worst consequence of British rule was not the economic degeneration we suffered, but the psychological and moral deterioration that had occurred. A European officer, even if he is the enemy, knows the value of freedom. No matter what façade he may put on for the sake of appearances, in his heart of hearts he cannot help but respect and acknowledge the soldiers of freedom. But it is not the same for an Indian who prides himself of being a foreign government's servant. This creature does not even know what freedom means. He has forgotten its fire, its sanctity. The heart and mind of this creature are no longer noble; they are made and controlled by a single spirit – the spirit of slavery!

9

The Lotus

It is the law of nature to intersperse the norm with the exception, the usual with the rare, the mundane with the remarkable. The lotus blooms surrounded by mud and an oasis occurs in an otherwise barren desert. Even in a place as inhuman as a prison, once in a while one is blessed by the unknown and mysterious workings of god's grace. Although I have just finished describing the cruelty and injustice that thrived within the jail walls, there were times when a pure soul appeared in our midst with warmth and decency etched on his face. My stint in jail was interspersed with the arrival (though infrequent) of people who still retained some notion of humanity, whose behaviour was always proper and kind. One such person whose presence always filled me with a strange mix of pride, surprise and joy, was an old warden of the prison. How I wish I could name him here in an acknowledgement of my gratitude and affection, but I know that by doing so I will create problems for that poor man.

One day as I sat in prison I was overcome by a feeling of deep disillusionment and disturbance. The old warden passed by and seeing me looking so distraught he sat down and started talking to me. 'Even though I have no complaints here,' I said, 'knowing that I am the only female political prisoner sometimes fills me with insecurity and apprehension.'

As soon as he heard this, he said, 'Behenji, don't worry on that score at all. If such a situation were ever to arise, I would not hesitate a second in sacrificing my job for you.'

He was not the kind of man who used big, bombastic words without meaning them. Even as he spoke I knew that each word came from the core of his heart. His face exuded the kind of aura that I have seen on the countenance of saints and men of integrity alone. Needless to say, after that conversation I never felt the need to worry about my security as long as I was in prison. I had learnt the lesson that even in a place as despairing as prison, the god above sends his angels of compassion to reassure and console us when we start doubting ourselves.

Then one day something else happened that filled me with an equal sense of wonder. By and large, a part of whatever fruits and other food came to the political prisoners of classes A and B got distributed among the wardens, jail workers, soldiers, etcetera. The lady warden always kept an eye on my things and almost every day I gave her a portion of whatever came for me.

On that particular day I came to know that the old warden was unwell. The doctor had told him to have milk and fruits but I knew that on his meagre salary of twenty rupees, and with a family to feed, he would not be able to afford that kind of diet. Deciding to help in the small way that I could, I told him to take my share of milk and fruits from that day onwards until he was better. But to my complete astonishment, he returned my food to me saying, 'Behenji, in all my life I have never eaten even at my elder sister's house. You are much younger than I am, and for a Hindu to eat the food that comes from his younger sister's house is a sin.'

Struck by the quiet dignity of that poor man, in that moment I realized how human nobility is sometimes found in the unlikeliest of places and in the most inconspicuous of people.

10

Falling Ill

Being locked up in my tiny cell within the four walls of the prison for days on end was bound to affect my health. Perhaps such a situation would not have been as intolerable to a woman who was used to staying within the confines of her home or remaining in purdah; but for someone like me, who had spent my entire life breathing in the air of freedom, growing up under the clear fresh sky of my beloved Kashmir, the condition proved oppressive beyond endurance. I would have managed to handle the psychological effects of my bondage in some way or the other, but it was not in my control to prevent its physical repercussions. The result was that after staying in prison for two months I started running a constant, nagging temperature that refused to go away. Each evening my fever would rise to a hundred degrees or so. After this had gone on for more that a fortnight and then for twenty days, I, and more than me, my family, started getting worried.

The question of consulting a lady doctor arose. I wanted Dr Mrs Tandon, whom I had been consulting so far, and made a request to the jail authorities to that effect. During those days an officer named Major Yule was in charge of the prison as Colonel Rehman was on leave for a week. He agreed to my request. However, when the warden came to know of this, he told Major Yule that Colonel Rehman would never have approved of sending for Mrs Tandon as there had been a disagreement between him and Captain Tandon over some issue. As a result Dr Tandon could not be called and finally, Major Yule brought a lady doctor called Miss John for my check-up. After a thorough medical examination, Miss John prescribed some medicines and left. The medicines arrived and I started taking them as per the prescription. But there was no one to see what effect – positive or negative – they were having on me. As per prison rules, once a bottle of medicine arrived the patient was supposed to continue taking it until it finished. And because of this lack of supervision, far from improving, my condition deteriorated.

This happened in the month of October. A few days later a European gentleman by the name of Mr Clyde succeeded Colonel Rehman as the superintendent of the prison. As I have mentioned earlier, he treated me with the utmost respect and consideration. On my husband's request, he even agreed to let me get a check-up by Meerut's well-known physician, Dr Bhopal Singhji. After this examination my family as well as I felt much more reassured and at ease than we had before.

Yet another favour granted to me was that I was allowed to go and consult a gynaecologist in Meerut city once every week. I remember the flood of emotions that overwhelmed me the first time I stepped out of the prison walls to go to the city. A lorry guarded by four armed policemen to counter any attempt at escape took me to the hospital concerned. Although I was surrounded by the state and police machinery on all sides, the opportunity of catching a glimpse of the streets of Meerut filled my heart with joy. How precious even an iota of freedom is to one deprived of it, I thought to myself. And how wondrously bright will be the day when my country wakes up to the dawn of freedom after centuries of slavery!

The lorry sped through the city. A number of times people I knew caught a glimpse of me. Many of them folded their hands in greeting, but before I could respond to the gestures, the vehicle had moved on. After spending around half an hour in hospital I returned to prison.

Initially, the day fixed for my hospital visits was Wednesday, but then, to do away with the possibility of potential sympathizers and supporters, the schedule was changed. Now there was no day fixed for the trips and I would suddenly be summoned out of the blue to leave at a minute's notice. Nevertheless, each week at least one medical examination was now certain, and I was soon able to feel a definite improvement in my condition. However, whether this improvement was because of the medicines prescribed by the doctors or because a person hitherto confined within the walls of prison was able to breathe in the open air, is not yet quite certain.

At this point I would like to make a few comments about the state of medical facilities in prison. I never had the opportunity to go to the jail medical ward myself, the prison doctor and compounder would come to the barrack to enquire about my health almost daily. According to the rules and regulations of prison, they were supposed to visit each of the prison wards every day. However, medical officers or doctors were rarely available for more than twenty or thirty days a year, and that too only during the outbreak of the malaria epidemic. Irrespective of whether the number of inmates in a barrack was 1000 or 400, a single doctor and his compounder were the only ones available and on their rounds. During the malaria epidemic a couple of other compounders arrived, but even they did not stay long. The reason for this, as it came to be known later, was that the new compounders were asked to work on a voluntary basis, i.e., without receiving any salary. No one was prepared to do this.

The state of the medicines was no better. A single bottle filled with a strange-looking fluid was supposed to be the cure for god knows how many illnesses. The bottles/medicines bore no name, only a number. I remember seeing a red liquid (which if I am not mistaken had the number 40 pasted on it) that was given to prisoners suffering from any kind of pain – be it a stomach ache, a headache, a muscle pull or a twisted ankle. At times the same liquid was poured into a measured cup and given to the patient for a cold or a cough as well.

Another thing I noticed was that the cloth used to cover the medicines and food that were brought for the patients was always extremely dirty. Every once in a while it would be washed by the compounder or orderly, but in a slipshod manner. If a patient managed to remain alive in such an environment it had more to do with luck rather than the facilities made available to him.

Added to this overall environment of unhygienic and ill-equipped infrastructure was a deep sense of indifference demonstrated by the so-called medical officers and representatives in the prison. Once, an elderly prisoner fell ill during the night. His condition deteriorated rapidly and one of his companions asked the warden to send for the compounder. Word was sent and the compounder informed. However, the response that came from there was this: 'If he is in such bad state, he'll probably be dead by the time I reach in any case. What is the point of my going all that way in the middle of the night for nothing? Just check if he's dead and put him on a separate bed.' The poor prisoner had fainted by now and was put on a separate bed. He kept lying there till eight o'clock the next morning, without anyone bothering to check if he was dead or alive. At exactly nine o'clock the superintendent entered the ward. He was informed that one of the prisoners had died at night. But when he removed the sheet from the corpse's body he saw that his heart was still beating. The prisoner was immediately picked up and brought inside the room but by now the chill of the night air had penetrated his bones and taken its toll. By afternoon the old prisoner was dead.

11

Special Guests

Some or the other of my Congress fellow-workers would usually visit me every fifteenth day. However, during my stay in prison, there were two occasions when I had 'special' guests who came to visit me in the barrack with the special permission of the superintendent.

One day Colonel Abdul Rehman came to my barrack. 'There are some British women who want to come and meet you in jail,' he said. 'Would you be willing to meet them or do you meet only Indian women?' The question as well as the sarcasm in his voice surprised me. Why would I have any objection to meeting anyone? Perhaps Colonel Rehman felt that we Congress people considered every Englishman an enemy; he did not understand that our grievances were not against any individual or class; they were against a policy of oppression and racism. In fact, harbouring bitterness in one's soul against any particular people was opposed to the very fundamentals of Mahatma Gandhi's teachings.

'Why should I have any objection to meeting a British woman?' I asked Colonel Rehman. 'On the contrary, being a woman she would be like a sister to me'.

Early the next morning the door to my ward opened. I was sitting in bed reading a book, and looked up to see Colonel Rehman walking towards my cell, accompanied by two women, one a European and the other an Indian. I got up and went outside my cell where the superintendent introduced us. The Indian woman was his wife and the European one was the wife of a British engineer stationed in Meerut. Mrs Rehman held out her hand towards me. Her first question was, 'Do you speak English?'

'Yes, I do.'

As soon as she heard this, a broad smile spread across her face. It was almost as if knowing how to speak in English was a matter of great pride. A feeling of sadness enveloped me as I realized that even for many of our own people, speaking the language of the oppressors in a land condemned to slavery was a matter of honour rather than shame.

I invited my visitors into my cell. All I had inside was an iron bed. There was no sitting arrangement. A small cane box in which I kept my food stood in the corner on a slab of mud. This was my entire household.

On another slab in the adjoining C-class barrack, the blankets and mats of the prisoners lay in a heap. Entering the barrack, Mrs Rehman came out immediately. 'Oh, this is very dirty,' she said.

She was right. After all how could a woman whose servants also lived in better accommodation, bear such living conditions? And she, being the superintendent's wife, was specially privileged.

I told her that I had no other seating arrangement to offer other than what she saw in front of her. Hearing this, the superintendent gestured to the prison attendants who carried in two chairs and a bench. Settling down the best that she could, Mrs Rehman asked me how long I had been in prison.

'From the eighteenth of July,' I answered.

'Were you occupying an important position in Meerut?' she

continued. I found this question rather strange and asked her what exactly she meant by it.

'I mean, were you a leader?'

I replied that I was one amongst many women who believed in and worked for the Congress. 'I used to tell my fellow countrymen to stop using foreign goods and to abstain from harmful substances like liquor. That is the crime for which I have been jailed.'

Mrs Rehman then seemed to notice the clothes I was wearing. 'This is khaddar,' she explained to the European woman with her, pointing to my sari.

'Why don't you also wear khadi?' I asked her, but she gave me no reply and went on to ask me where in Meerut I lived.

Replying to her question in a perfunctory manner I came back to my initial line of questioning.

'You are also an Indian. Why don't you also join the Congress?'

'How can I do that?' Mrs Rehman replied. 'My husband is a government official.'

'So what?' I persisted. 'There are many women in Meerut whose husbands work for the government but who have joined us. They play a very active part in helping us. After all, there are many ways of extending support to your country.'

I think Mrs Rehman did not like what I said and she soon left the cell. The next day the doctor who used to come for my check-up asked me what I had said to her. I wanted to know why he was asking this. 'Colonel Rehman was saying that you asked his wife to wear khadi and to help the Congress,' he replied. 'Is that true?'

'Yes, it is,' I said. 'I certainly said so. What is the harm in it?'

The meeting I have described above was of one sort. In complete contrast to this was the meeting I had with an Irish woman who came to meet me a few days later. In the first meeting the woman who had come to meet me was an Indian. But she had not come to me out of any sense of support or sympathy; she was not in the least concerned with either my happiness or sadness. For her I merely presented an opportunity to see a female political leader in prison, a creature behind bars to be looked down on and scorned at.

The Irish woman, in contrast, was not motivated by such reasons. She came with genuine concern and love in her heart. She had not come to view the woman in prison as a spectacle, to scoff at her. She had come simply to see the person behind the image – she had come to meet Urmila.

I was running a fever in those days. I had not been notified of her visit and was lying in bed. Suddenly the door opened. I saw a European woman enter the compound with the superintendent. As soon as I recognized her, I sat up in joy and excitement. She was Mrs O'Donnell, an old acquaintance of mine and the wife of the principal of Meerut College where my husband taught.

Mrs O'Donnell came up to me and shook my hand warmly. Once again I was assailed by the same thoughts I had had earlier – where should I make my visitor sit. However, as if reading my thoughts, she put my apprehensions to rest. 'This is not your home, Urmila,' she said. 'Why are you bothering about such formalities?'

Both of us sat down on the hard iron bed and started talking. She asked me all about myself, about my health, and the way I spent my time. Such was the warmth that emanated from her that I felt as if I was well again.

There were a lot of mosquitoes in the cell, but she did not complain even once. After a while, and only when I had commented on them myself, did she ask me the reason for their presence in such large numbers.

'Every eighth day the walls of the cell are plastered with mud,' I explained to her. 'The mud that the authorities bring for this purpose is very dirty. From the stink, I think they get it from the nearby drain. As soon as it dries, mosquitoes and flies start swarming around. I don't know how many other insects, some of them an inch long, live in that mud. When I started getting fever I requested the authorities not to use that mud for plastering the walls, but my requests had no effect. I even sent for a mosquito net from home. But since it is of khadi, the air does not pass through it easily. Each time I used it I felt suffocated and had to keep it away. I'm sure that the mosquito menace is one of the biggest problems that prisoners face in jail. Sometimes I think that the insects also conspire with the government to add to our discomfort and give us yet another reason to fear the prisons.'

For a long time Mrs O'Donnell and I kept talking. After she left, a strange emptiness descended on me. The memories of the time I spent with her and the genuine affection and concern she extended to me continued to warm my heart for a long time to come.

12

The End of Solitude

Although there were always two or three women present in my ward, their presence was of no comfort to me. They were not the kind of women I could exchange ideas or have conversations with. I am sure that even if I had been kept with completely illiterate village women I would have found something to talk to them about, to develop a congenial familiarity with. But the women I was kept with were completely different, the kind whom one rarely if ever meets. They had been caught committing murders and robberies and were not at all ashamed of their past actions. It was not revulsion but fear that they inspired in me, and as far as possible I kept to myself. For almost three months after coming to the prison I spent my time all alone. Usually it was only those convicted of serious crimes who were sentenced to solitary confinement, but in an ironic twist of fate, I suffered the condition even in the normal course of my sentence.

Initially, I consoled myself by saying that sooner or later my companions in the struggle outside would also join me. But days, weeks and then months passed without that coming to pass. It was not that after my arrest the women workers of the Congress had stopped their activities. In fact, just the day after my arrest they had carried out agitations and picketing that were enough for them to have been arrested and imprisoned. What had changed, it seems, was the policy of the government, which now felt that further arrests would only aggravate the situation. Political workers were therefore not being arrested with the same frequency that they had been earlier.

A day before my arrest I had made the following statement in my speech: 'One does not get sent to prison for the sake of one's motherland simply by sedition or picketing or the boycott of foreign goods. It is only when destiny smiles on you that this reward is granted.'

I had been actively involved in all kinds of protests against the government for almost three months before my arrest. Speeches, demonstrations, picketing, and bonfires of foreign goods – I had done them all, but no action was ever taken. And when the moment finally came, I was arrested for something as trivial as asking college students to become Congress volunteers! When the magistrate had asked me if I had 'incited' students to picket shops, I had laughed in his face and said that I had done much more than that.

The arrest or non-arrest of persons depended entirely on the whims of the government. Those who were arrested told themselves that the government had finally realized their value (also seen as the potential threat they held). In such an environment, when no other arrests were made after mine, it was difficult to decide whether it was I – inside the prison – who was more blessed than those outside or vice versa.

However, my days of solitude soon came to an end. On the twelfth of October, my prison-home was graced by the presence of my fellow Congress workers who had also been arrested for their crime of demanding freedom for their motherland. Two of these women had been my companions in organizing and carrying out the boycott of foreign goods. Their names were Prakashwati and Vidya Devi. The third woman was Kamala Devi Chowdhrani, who was the president of Meerut's Women's Charkha Committee. It will not be possible for my readers to understand the kind of joy and elation that filled my heart the day these fellow soldiers of the freedom movement came to join me in my barrack; after all, the respite of shade is known only to those who have walked far and long in the sweltering heat of the burning sun. For me, their presence was like rain after a drought, like wealth after deprivation, like food after starvation. That day was a day of celebration for me and there were many who congratulated me at having finally received the antidote to my lonely days in prison.

As expected, the jail authorities arrived to make a show of their concern and good intentions. The jailor, who had come to the barrack on some lame pretext, was one such official.

'Technically the new prisoners have not yet been designated their class,' he said, 'but I will have the A-class food sent for them in any case, so that they do not have any problem.'

The 'class' of a prisoner is usually decided at the time of sentencing, which is why, until the final hearing in a case, the final 'class' cannot be designated. But apprehensive of the consequences of any ill-treatment of women political prisoners in prison, the authorities had taken a decision to categorize all female political prisoners as A class. Either the jailor was not aware of this or he was feigning ignorance deliberately.

But the women were not in the least impressed by his tactic. 'Our class has been designated,' said Vidyawatiji. 'Please arrange for our beds to be sent here.'

'Which beds are you talking about?' asked the jailor in surprise.

'My bed must be lying somewhere in the A-class male ward,' Vidyawatiji replied without batting an eyelid. 'It had been sent from home when my husband was here but now that he has been transferred to another jail it should be available. And for my other companions you can always send for beds from their houses.'

Thus snubbed, the jailor stared at her. 'There are no beds for C-class prisoners,' he snapped at her and walked away. However, after being harassed for a few days, the new prisoners were finally provided with beds.

The superintendent also made a round to acquaint himself with the new additions to his prison. All of us were in the barrack kitchen when he arrived and the sweeper called us out. Walking up to the women, Colonel Rehman asked them their names, their addresses and their reasons for being in prison. Having finished with Vidyawatiji and Prakashwatiji he moved to Kamalaji and asked her name.

'Kamala Devi Chowdhrani,' came the reply.

'Your husband's name?'

'Dr Chowdhary.'

'Are you a Bengali?'

'No, we belong to Lucknow.'

'Where did your husband get his degree from?'

'From Calcutta.'

'If you are not Bengalis why did he get his degree from Calcutta? Why not from Lucknow?'

'I cannot answer that question. You will have to ask him.'

At the last reply, a frown creased the superintendent's forehead. 'Ask him?' he repeated, sensing the irreverence in the tone of the woman he was questioning. Turning around, he left the ward abruptly, but we could make out that his anger had been provoked. As a result, Kamala Devi's visiting rights were suspended and were resumed only a few days later, that too after a lot of effort.

A discussion of this behaviour seems useless. Perhaps it is only a psychiatrist who can explain the strange workings of insecurity and aggression in a man who imagines disrespect in a neutral reply and then proceeds to extract a perverse revenge from his assumed culprit.

After the twelfth of October my lonely existence in jail came to an end. Now the strains of the national song could be heard here as well, the sounds of conversations and laughter resounded from its walls too. Yet, once in a while I was roused by feelings of guilt that after the advent of my human companions I had started neglecting the trees and the birds that had for so long been my only companions and soulmates.

13

Food in the Prison

The food cooked in prison was the same for everyone, but A-class prisoners were allowed to send for food from home. The Jail Manual said that we could 'supplement' our meals by sending for extra food from home, but the meaning of the word 'supplement' depended on the whims and moods of the prison officials. Sometimes they took it to mean only fruits and at other times they extended its scope to other things. For about a week after I arrived in prison I was given the food cooked there. After that, in order to avoid unnecessary complications, I took permission to cook myself. That is when I came to know the exact proportion of food we prisoners were allowed.

Those of us who had been sentenced to ordinary imprisonment were allowed uncooked food worth six annas per day; for those sentenced to 'rigorous imprisonment' this was increased to eight annas. From the time I started to cook for myself, each morning my rations were measured out in the following quantities:

1 *chataak* milk
3 *tola* rice (later raised to 5)
1 *chataak* potatoes
2 *chataak* daal

½ *chataak* bura
6 *chataak* ground wheat
½ *ser* wood (for burning)
a bit of salt
a bit of chilli powder and other basic condiments
½ *tola* tea

During the last two months of my term when I was unwell, I received extra milk, bread, butter and potatoes in addition to the above mentioned portions.

The food that the C-class prisoners received was extremely bad. Their chapattis would be half cooked, burnt and full of sand grains that had been used to adulterate the flour. Sometimes we asked prisoners in that category to give us a little of their food to get an idea of how different it was from our own. Needless to say, most of their food was inedible. The oil would be raw, the chilly content too high. According to the Jail Manual, the prison doctor was required to be present at the time the food was cooked but this instruction was never followed. The doctor passed on the responsibility to the compounder, who overburdened as he was never fulfilled it. There was just one compounder between thousands of prisoners. He had to distribute the daily rounds of medicines and hardly had the time to fulfil this additional responsibility that had been unfairly dumped on him. The result was that both areas of his responsibility suffered – neither did the patients receive their medicines on time nor was the cooking of food supervised properly. But yes, whenever a senior officer came on inspection, the doctor made it a point to be available and ensure all requirements of the Jail Manual were complied with. The Jail Manual also said that whatever vegetables were grown in the prison garden were to be used for the prisoners. However, this never happened, specially for C-class prisoners. It was believed that the vegetables found their way into the kitchens of the prison workers. In an amazing coincidence, each time fresh cauliflower was plucked for the day's meal, the flower disappeared before reaching the kitchen and all that appeared in cooked form was the thick stems of the vegetable that remained. The daal cooked for C-class prisoners would inevitably be black in colour and the chapattis managed the incredible feat of being raw and burnt at the same time.

The high level of adulteration in the flour used to make the chapattis can be explained. Each prisoner was given a fixed number of five chapattis each day. For the ordinary prisoners this was enough, but for those sentenced to vigorous imprisonment, who spent the entire day grinding wheat and doing hard labour, this was not sufficient. As a result, these men ate the flour while they were grinding it and filled their stomachs as much as they could. However, there was one problem in this arrangement. When they handed in the flour it was weighed; if it was discovered to be less the men would get into serious trouble. So, to cover up, the men mixed the flour with *real*, a fine form of sand that looks like flour. This added both weight and quantity to the flour. Soon this method started being used by the prison officials as well. They added *real* to the flour when they bought it from the market. This cost less and they were able to pocket the extra money. Consequently, the chapattis in prison were always full of unhealthy and at times even risky irritants.

A far as the vegetable called 'bhujiya' is concerned, the less said about it the better. This particular concoction was so unique in its preparation and insipidity that I will have to dedicate an entire chapter to its description. I think I'll leave that for later.

14

Class Discrimination in Prison

It was the death of the country's beloved martyr Yatindradas that finally jerked the British government out of its otherwise stone-hearted and complacent indifference. It took nothing less than the sacrifice of his life to make the authorities realize that the inhuman treatment being meted out to political prisoners all over the country was far from the ideals so proudly proclaimed by the stalwarts of the Empire. After an investigation into the matter it was decided that apart from ordinary prisoners, all political prisoners were to be divided into different categories called 'classes', with the A and the B classes to be provided with a set of facilities that were not extended to the others. Rules were passed to secure them with certain privileges and special treatment that the class C prisoners were deprived of. In retrospect, the true intention behind these new rules appears clear – they were just another opportunity for the British to put into practice their vile but effective policy of divide and rule.

There are ample examples to show how popular and respected leaders were often condemned to the B class without any reason, and deprived of those facilities that they deserved and would have received had they been in the A class. The authorities believed that by this kind of discrimination they would be able to evoke feelings of resentment and foster differences amongst the otherwise united satyagrahis. In addition to this, those in the C class were incited against their leaders by being told that while they were suffering, A - and B-class prisoners were leading comfortable lives in their cells, provided with food and facilities that were beyond their imagination. The truth was far removed from this convoluted impression that the authorities tried to create. On many occasions, the satyagrahis in the A and B classes put in applications for transfers to the C category, with the intention of experiencing what their companions in the lower categories had to go through. However, this would have been in direct contradiction of the selfishness that the government wanted to project on the satyagrahi leaders. Therefore, far from accepting these applications, the authorities did not even acknowledge them.

It should also not be assumed that the 'A' and 'B' class prisoners were given all the facilities that the Jail Manual said they had a right to. The dispensation of those 'rights' depended entirely on the will of the jail workers and officials. They were provided in full in some prisons, very little in others, extended in some and denied completely in others.

The first thing I had asked for on arriving in prison was paper. Although class-A prisoners are entitled to get paper if they wanted, I had to wait a long time for my request to be granted, and that too, after much reminding and discussion. At one time things between the authorities and me became so strained that the jailor sent me a message saying that prisoners will be allowed only enough paper to write letters twice a week. Other than that, no extra demands for paper would be entertained. But I must admit that I was finally given a notebook to write in.

At this point it would not be inappropriate for me to mention another privilege that was extended to me by Colonel Rehman. The heat in Meerut during the months of July and August was oppressive in its intensity. In that sweltering weather I had to sleep in a closed room without any ventilation or fan. Seeing my condition, the superintendent it seems was moved to pity; he allowed me to send for a kerosene-run table fan from home. This perhaps is the only example of the superintendent's kindness towards me in the entire duration of my stay in prison. Ironically, the concerned fan never helped appease my discomfort – the sound it made while running, the stink the kerosene emitted, and its frequent malfunctioning all led to it being redundant for all practical purposes.

Being a member of the class-A prisoner group had yet another disadvantage. We were asked to send for everything we required from our homes. Theoretically this was against the rules as political prisoners were supposed to be provided with certain facilities, but practically, this rule was never applied. Even the oil in our lamps was not filled by the authorities – we had to send for it ourselves.

There was another problem that we faced in our barrack. It had become home to a number of pigeons that had made their nests there. Anyone who has seen the state of prisons would know that there are ample niches in their ceilings for birds and insects to make their homes. As a result, the nests were on the ceiling and our beds on the floor, directly below them. Because of this our beds would get soiled by pigeon droppings, feathers, bits of grain and sometimes even with broken eggs from fallen nests almost every day. There was not a single piece of clothing or bedding that had not been spoiled by pigeon droppings, and we were constantly washing them. The prisoners made repeated requests to the authorities but nothing happened. Once when the collector was on an inspection round I showed him my clothes which had got soiled just a few minutes before his arrival. Looking at me passively he said, 'Mrs Shastri, if we have any funds left over from the prison funds we'll see if we can do anything about the ceiling.' That was the last we ever heard him mention the subject. In later years whenever someone was released from prison, I made it a point to ask about the ceiling. The answers were always the same – there was no improvement, nothing had changed.

If this was the condition of the A- and B-class prisoners, one can well imagine how bad things must have been for those in the C class. The prisoners there had to agitate and resort to a fast unto death for every little demand to be given a fair hearing, let alone granted. And in most cases, though fasting yielded results for those in the former categories, they served only to worsen conditions for the latter. Any prisoner resorting to this means usually ended up in solitary confinement with vigorous punishment.

There was one particular incident when a group of women were arrested under suspicion for attempted theft in the fair of Garhmukteshwar. At that time there was only one toilet in our barrack and as expected, it soon became very dirty. I requested the warden to make an alternate arrangement but despite repeated requests nothing was done to improve the situation. When four days passed without any action I sent a message to the jailor through the warden, saying that if no alternate arrangement was made by the end of that day, I would have no option other than resorting to a hunger strike. After a while the warden returned with the following reply: 'If you do so, the jailor shall have no option other than transferring you to another jail.'

'All right,' I replied with firm resolve. 'In that case, please inform the jailor that as of now I am on a hunger strike and shall continue until my demands have been met.'

Convinced that I was serious in my intentions and apprehensive of having a politically problematic situation on his hands, the jailor was forced into action. By the end of the day the arrangement for another toilet had been made.

One of the biggest advantages of being an A-class prisoner, in my opinion, was that I was allowed to write and send letters and meet visitors twice a month. These privileges meant a lot to me and offered me great respite specially during the first three months when I was alone in the ward.

All things considered, I am convinced that the class differences practised by the authorities were not only extremely damaging to us as a nation, but were also politically detrimental. Because educated and aware people were put into A and B classes, C-class prisoners had to face innumerable difficulties. Since most of them were not even aware of the rights, their ignorance was exploited to the maximum. It is therefore no surprise that a lot of these prisoners were filled with discontent and resentment against their leaders, something that was not only encouraged but even provoked by the government and prison authorities.

I am certain that if class distinctions imposed by the government were to be removed and all prisoners considered a part of the same class, it would serve as a great advantage to our nation and its people. More than half the problems of C-class prisoners would end if they were kept in the same manner and as part of the same category as A- and B-class prisoners. The Congress dreams of a swarajya, in which there is no discrimination of any sort, in which all people – rich and poor alike – live in equality, partaking of the same privileges and problems. And if we believe that jail is but a means to that larger, greater end, why shouldn't it exemplify that very world we wish to live in someday, that very swarajya which is our life's aim.

I therefore feel that the Congress must make every attempt to ensure that all forms of class discrimination should end. We must make a focused and concerted effort to struggle towards that end.

15

Release

Very often while I was in prison, I heard rumours of my early release based on my illness. Five months had already passed. At times I heard that because of volunteering in work that had not been binding on me, my chances for an early release had increased. But even now, no clear date had been announced.

One day during the daily parade I heard my history ticket being sent for. This was a kind of file that contained details of a prisoner – medical, political, criminal, professional, legal. When it was returned, I saw that the date of my release, previously fixed for the second of January, had been struck out and replaced by another date. The new date was sixth of January. For some strange reason my sentence had been extended by four days.

I can think of no one who does not look forward to returning home. It is a trait basic to human nature. Irrespective of whatever luxuries are afforded, and even after staying in the best possible places, there comes a moment when one is suddenly overwhelmed by homesickness and a longing for one's own family. That I suppose is the reason why men go insane in palaces no less than in mud houses.

Those were days when memories of home exerted a pull stronger than they had ever done before. The words 'east or west, home is the best' seemed to have been written specially for me, and my identification with them was so great that I even embroidered them on the corner of my pillowcase. In those days I craved for home the way a devotee craves for a glimpse of god. I kept imagining how things would be the day I would be released from prison – how my name would be announced, how my relatives and loved ones would gather to welcome me, how I would walk up to the main gate of the prison and walk out of it into a world without walls. Days in which I would be free again, days when I would walk unguarded by soldiers.

Sometimes I felt that my condition was no different from that of a caged bird – a bird that longs for her nest beyond the bars of her cage, a nest that she had built for her family, one twig, one straw at a time. She flaps her wings in an attempt to break free, but the guard outside her cage makes sure there is no way of escape and leaves her to suffer her loneliness and agony alone. Like many times before, I was reminded of some lines written by the famous poet Iqbal:

I think once again of that time passed away,
The shrubs in my courtyard, my nest, my home.
How we would soar together in the free skies above,
With winds and clouds to lift us,
Our wings spread out wide and free.
The desire in my heart is to fly that way once more,
To perch on the treetops, to sing songs of freedom.
Once more on the branch of that tree,
My destroyed nest I wish to bring back to life.

Finally the day I was waiting for arrived. However, in a strange twist of irony, my family as well as I were completely unaware of its arrival. The reason for this was that while my release was expected on the sixth of January, I was set free on the third.

Kamala, one of my companions in prison, was unwell. At around nine o'clock I spread out her mattress in the portion of our barrack where the sunlight was strongest and helped her lie down. Just then the door opened. A sweeper entered. Addressing me in his usual manner he said, 'Come on, Urmilaji, let's go.' Since the time of my illness I often went for my medical check-ups at this time. But today? I was completely confused. Despite asking the jailor to allow me to visit the doctor for the last eleven days, my requests had been repeatedly turned down. That must be the reason, I thought to myself. They've finally agreed to take me to the hospital. Turning to the warden I said, 'All these days when I asked you take me to a doctor you kept refusing, and today, without any intimation you decide to take me there just like that. I will not go. Now I will leave this cell only to go home.'

Looking at me with a slightly amused expression on his face, the warden replied, 'But that's exactly what you are being called for. To go home.' For a moment I could not believe my ears. And then, as comprehension dawned I turned to hear the warmth-filled voices of my companions. 'So Behenji,' Kamala Devi said, 'it seems that today you will be leaving us and moving on.'

'Please hurry up,' the warden interrupted. 'Your servant is waiting at the main entrance.'

Hearing this I was even more surprised. Did that mean that no one apart from my servant had arrived to take me home? With great effort I turned to him. 'Has no one else come? I asked.

'No,' he replied, and then continued, 'In fact, Urmilaji, even he had come only to collect your dirty clothes for washing. But the sahib said that we should release you today itself, so we felt you could return with him.'

How strange I felt. The same barrack where I had spent the last five and a half months, where I had lived through half the summer, all the monsoon and half the winter, had become out of limits for me in a split second; now I did not even have the right to stand here for a moment longer than I was allowed to. I still do not remember how my things got packed, how my bed got rolled. All I remember is my companions, my sisters in struggle, bidding me goodbye with warmth, smiles and laughter.

I came outside to the door near the barrack. The main gate was surrounded by policemen and wardens. I could see my servant Govardhan standing outside, waiting for me. Coming up to me, the warden told me that I had been called upstairs by superintendent sahib. Accompanied by him, I started climbing the stairs.

'So, Urmilaji,' Superintendent Rehman asked me once I had entered, 'how are you?'

'I am well, thank you,' I replied.

'Ready to leave prison, I'm sure.'

'Yes, let's see when I make my next trip here.'

Taken aback at my reply, Colonel Rehman looked at me in surprise. 'What did you say,' he asked, 'do you intend to be back here again?'

Turning back, I replied with a slight smile, 'Perhaps.'

I came downstairs accompanied by the assistant jailor. Here I was told to wait until my luggage was checked before I could be allowed to leave. Standing near the main table I kept waiting, with the jail workers passing by me every few minutes. Finally, after having waited for over an hour and driven to the end of my patience, I told the warden that since I was not free to leave, I should be sent to the women's ward until he had the time to attend to my case. Even as I was speaking, the superintendent came out of his room. Seeing me still standing there, he asked the jailor why I had not yet been released. 'Sir, her luggage has to be checked first,' he answered. Gesturing towards a chair standing in the corner, the superintendent asked me sit down while I waited. Then, turning around abruptly, he left.

The jailor asked for my luggage to be sent to his office where each item was checked and rechecked by the prison staff. I knew that it was a futile exercise as there was nothing to be found. The only things I had with me were a few letters sent by Professorji, a photograph of him and another of a little girl. These things were put aside on the jailor's table.

I had a small diary as well in which I used to write things that came to my mind or those that I had read and had thought worth making a note of. There was nothing in that diary that could prove harmful for the authorities even if it left the prison. Most of the pages had been used for writing applications, but despite that, perhaps just to harass me, the diary was also taken out and placed on the table. The authorities took more than an hour in carrying out an unnecessary and tedious search of me. The photographs were returned to me but all my letters, even though they bore the signature of the superintendent allowing them to enter the prison, were confiscated.

I could not understand this. When the officer in charge of the prison had himself allowed my letters to pass through the gates, on what grounds could they be held back from me now? According to the rule book the jailor had absolutely no right to hold back my letters, but despite my arguments all he said was that they would be returned to me after getting them sanctioned by sahib once again.

This new turn of events put me in a real dilemma. My letters were no longer in my possession and my soul refused to return home without them. These were the very letters that I had gone over innumerable times during my days in prison; I had loved them, revered them, gone over each word contained in them with no less devotion than that of worship. As I left the prison that day, those letters from my husband were my sole and sacred valuables. Seeing the expression on my face the jailor was finally moved enough to offer me some reassurance. 'Please don't worry, Urmilaji,' he said. 'I shall keep them very carefully. I'll make sure they reach you as soon as sir gives permission, and in case permission is denied I promise you I will burn them with my own hands. No one else will ever read them.' Left with no option, I closed my eyes in disappointment and came out of the prison office alone and empty-handed.

A few minutes later, at exactly 11:30 a.m. the gate of the prison opened. Walking up to me the jailor said, 'All right, Mrs Shastri, you are now free to go. Please forgive any mistakes that might have been made by us while you were here.' With these words he escorted me to a tonga waiting outside. Once all my things – bed, box and bag – were loaded, there was no place left for me to sit. As luck would have it, at just that moment a car going towards the city happened to be passing by. I requested its occupants to give me a ride and they agreed willingly. 'God be with you,' said the jailor as he closed the door behind me with a gesture of finality.

The car sped in the direction of my home. The route it took was the same that I used to take every eight days for my medical check-up, but unlike on those days, today the sky seemed to be a brighter shade of blue, resplendent and warm. Even now I could hardly believe that after all these days I was finally on my way home. Behind me, the carriage carrying my luggage evoked considerable interest amongst the passers-by on the road. People peeped out of windows, stared out of shops to get a better look. One man who happened to catch a glimpse of me in the car shouted to the others in excitement, 'Urmilaji has been released!' Some passengers who were about to board a lorry standing nearby turned back to make sure if what they had heard was correct. 'Behenji, namaste!' one of them said.

As the car turned the corner I caught my first glimpse of my house in six months. From a distance I could make out the verandah and the vague shapes of people standing there. With each step my heart lurched within me; for a second I almost felt as if my soul would leave my body and rush ahead. With each moment, a gamut of feelings jostled within me, merging into each other, joining and separating in new and hitherto unexperienced combinations of joy and pain and anticipation and a delayed sorrow at the separation endured.

Moving in a zombie-like state I lost all consciousness of my actions and myself. Finally reality sank it and my consciousness absorbed it bit by beautiful bit. Five minutes later as I looked around, I found myself sitting in the same room where six months ago, I had sat preparing to leave for my term in prison.

About the translator

Dr. Sonal Parmar has been working as an independent writing and editorial consultant for the last ten years. She has taught at Indraprastha and Ramjas Colleges, Delhi University, and has been associated with the National School of Drama, New Delhi, for the last 5 years, as consultant editor and editor-in-chief of all its international festival-related publications. She has been associated with NGOs and individuals on different projects as well as with several institutions such as Carnegie Hall (New York), Mind & Life (Zurich), India Habitat Centre (New Delhi), National Human Rights Commission (New Delhi), Sanatan (Varanasi), and Indira Gandhi National Centre for the Arts (New Delhi) in editorial and production/organizational capacities. Some of the books edited by her are *Let There Be Light* by Mahesh Nair, *Science and Spirituality* by Prof. Pranab Das, Elon University, *The Indian Art Collectors Handbook* by Dr. Alka Pande, *Swayamsiddha*, a book on the art of painter-sculptor Seema Kohli, and *Sculptures of Ram Kinker Baij* by K.S Radhakrishnan. She has translated into English *Lal Kothi Alvida,* a novel by Sharat Kumar which was serialized by Balraj Sahni Productions for Doordarshan.

कारागार

कारागार

जेल-जीवन का आन्तरिक चित्र

स्वर्गीया श्रीमती उर्मिला शास्त्री

प्रस्तावना

श्रीमती कस्तूरीबाई गान्धी

त्यागमूर्ति
श्रद्धेय श्रीयुत जमनालाल जी बजाज
के
कर कमलों में
सादर उपहार

जिस यात्रा की यह कहानी है, उस मार्ग पर चलने की प्रथम प्रेरणा आप ही के द्वारा मेरे हृदय में उत्पन्न हुई थी।

—**उर्मिला**

प्रस्तावना

बहन उर्मिलादेवी शास्त्री ने अपने जेल के अनुभवों की यह सुन्दर पुस्तक लिखी है, उसके लिए मैं उनका अभिनन्दन करती हूँ। विवाह के बाद पति के साथ गृहस्थाश्रम व्यतीत करने की बड़ी उत्कट इच्छा को ले कर वे मेरठ आयी थीं। परन्तु देश की .ख़तिर उन्होंने उस सुख को छोड़ कर जेल के सुख को सहर्ष स्वीकार किया। इस युद्ध में अखिल भारत की बहनों ने चारों तरफ़ ऐसा ही त्याग, ऐसी ही देश-भक्ति और ऐसी ही बहादुरी दिखा कर हिन्दुस्तान की स्त्री-जाति को गौरवान्वित किया है।

जो बहनें जेल जा कर आयी हैं, उन्हें इस पुस्तक को पढ़ कर अपने जेल-जीवन के दिन पुनः स्मरण हो उठेंगे। जिन बहनों को बहन उर्मिला की भाँति जेल जाने का सौभाग्य मिला न होगा वे इस बहन की ईर्ष्या करेंगी!! परन्तु मैं जानती हूँ कि केसरी साड़ी परिधान धारण करने वाली देश सेविकाओं ने शराब की, विदेशी कपड़े की दुकानों पर शान्त पहरे लगाने में कुछ कम कष्ट सहन नहीं किये, कुछ कम बहादुरी नहीं दिखलायी। बहुतेरी देश सेविकाओं ने तो जेल के दुःखों को भी फीका करने वाले कठोर दुःख सहन कर दिखाये हैं और मैं स्वयं ऐसी बहनों की साक्षी हूँ।

बहन उर्मिला देवी ने ऐसी सरल और सरस हिन्दी में यह पुस्तक लिखी है कि मुझे उसे समझने में तनिक भी मुश्किल नहीं पड़ी, अतः मैं बहन उर्मिला को उसके लिए .खास बधाई देती हूँ।

सत्याग्रहाश्रम
साबरमती

—कस्तूरीबाई गाँधी

'कारागार': एक प्रतिवेदन

पूज्य माता स्वर्गीया कस्तूरबा ने इस पुस्तक के प्रथम संस्करण की प्रस्तावना में लिखा था--"जो बहनें जेल जा कर आयी हैं, उन्हें इस पुस्तक को पढ़ कर अपने जेल-जीवन के दिन पुनः स्मरण हो उठेंगे? जिन बहनों को बहन उर्मिलाजी की भाँति जेल जाने का सौभाग्य मिला न हो, वे इस बहन से ईर्ष्या करेंगी!! परन्तु मैं जानती हूँ कि केसरी साड़ी पहने देश सेविकाओं ने शराब को, विदेशी कपड़े की दुकानों पर शान्त पहरे लगाने में कुछ कम कष्ट सहन नहीं किये। कुछ कम बहादुरी नहीं दिखलायी। बहुत-सी बहनों ने तो जेल के दुखों को भी फीका करने वाले कठोर दुःख सहन कर दिखाये हैं।"

जब यह पुस्तक छपी थी तभी वह मेरे पास 'विशाल भारत' में समालोचनार्थ आयी थी और मैंने उसे पढ़ा भी था, पर उसकी याद मैं बिलकुल भूल चुका था। हाँ, इस बीच एक बार स्वर्गीय उर्मिला की बड़ी बहन सत्यवतीजी ने 'विशाल भारत' के शहीद अंक में उनको श्रद्धांजलि अवश्य अर्पित की थी।

इस बार जब उक्त पुस्तक की पुरानी खण्डित प्रति मुझे फिर मिली तो नेत्र ज्योति मन्द होने पर भी मैं तन्मयता के साथ पढ़ गया। मैं यह ईमानदारी के साथ स्वीकार करूँगा कि पुस्तक पढ़ जाने पर मुझे इस बात से घोर लज्जा का अनुभव हुआ कि जिस स्वाधीनता की प्राप्ति के लिए हमारी हज़ारों ही बहनों को इतनी भयंकर यातनाएँ भोगनी पड़ीं, उसके संघर्ष में भाग लेने का कोई भी सौभाग्य मुझे प्राप्त नहीं हुआ जबकि उसके शुभ परिणाम मैंने पूर्ण मात्रा में भोगे।

दूसरा विचार जो मेरे मन में उत्पन्न हुआ, वह यह था कि इस महत्त्वपूर्ण दस्तावेज़ का द्वितीय संस्करण इतने वर्ष तक क्यों अप्रकाशित पड़ा रहा। हिन्दी

जगत की वर्तमान परिस्थिति तो इसके लिए ज़िम्मेवार है ही, पर साथ-ही-साथ हम लोगों का भी अपराध कम नहीं है।

मुझे बहन उर्मिलाजी के कुटुम्बियों से भली-भाँति परिचित होने का सौभाग्य ४०-५० वर्ष से प्राप्त है। डॉ. धर्मेन्द्रनाथ शास्त्री जी के प्रथम दर्शन मुझे अपने नगर फ़िरोज़ाबाद में ही हुए थे, जबकि वे वृन्दावन गुरुकुल से स्नातक हो कर स्थानीय आर्यसमाज में पधारे थे, उनके भाषण से मैं भी इतना प्रभावित हुआ था कि रात बारह बजे उन्हें स्टेशन पर पहुँचाने गया था। बहन उर्मिलाजी के प्रथम दर्शन मेरठ में ही हुए थे। तत्पश्चात बहन सत्यवती तथा अन्य बहनों से परिचय हुआ।

इस पुस्तक के तो कई संस्करण अब तक छप जाने चाहिएँ थे। यह उन दिनों की याद दिलाती है जब हमारा देश पराधीन था। इसमें कई अध्यायों, मसलन 'ख़ून के आँसू' को तो पाठ्य पुस्तकों में उद्धृत करना चाहिए था। उसमें जेल में बालकों पर बेंत पड़ने का हृदय-बेधक वर्णन है।

जेल में ख़ूबसूरत लड़कियों के साथ जो अनाचार किये जाते हैं, उनका उल्लेख पढ़ कर हृदय काँप उठता है। हृदयहीन लेडी वॉर्डरों के ज़ुल्म पढ़ कर क्रोध आता है। और जेल के नालायक भारतीय सुप्रिण्टेण्डेण्ट के कारनामे तो और भी उद्वेगकारी हैं। मेरा एक सुझाव है—वह यह है कि हिन्दी में एक वृहत ग्रन्थ छापा जाये जिसमें स्वाधीनता संग्राम में भाग लेने वाली महिलाओं के अनुभव संग्रह कर दिये जायें। उनमें बहुत-सी तो स्वर्गवासी हो चुकी हैं, पर कितनी अब भी विद्यमान हैं– जैसे श्रीमती कृष्णा देवी गो सेविका (फ़र्रुख़ाबाद) और श्रीमती ताराrानी श्रीवास्तव (महाराजगंज सारन, बिहार), श्रीमती फूलमती देवी, इत्यादि। उस पुस्तक को भी पूज्य माता कस्तूरबा की पवित्र समृति को अर्पित कर देना ठीक होगा। भूमिका में दक्षिण अफ्रीका की उन बहनों, कुमारी लि-अम्मा अथवा सुरेदाई सेलवन का भी उल्लेख होना चाहिए जो इस हेतु शहीद हुई थीं, जिससे यह स्मृति ग्रन्थ का रूप धारण कर ले। बहन सत्यवतीजी इस पुण्य कार्य को आसानी से कर सकती हैं। इस वृहत ग्रन्थ – "स्वाधीनता संग्राम में भारतीय स्त्रियों का योगदान" की योजना भी उनकी देख-रेख में तैयार हो सकती है। स्वर्गीय जमनालाल जी के वंशज तथा भाई सीताराम सेक्सरिया इस यज्ञ में भरपूर सहायता दे सकते हैं। बहन उर्मिला जी ने केवल 33 वर्ष की ही उम्र पायी। इस छोटी-सी उम्र में भी उन्होंने बहुत-से काम किये, जिनका उल्लेख इस पुस्तक के

प्रारम्भ में कर दिया है। केवल आत्मचरित की दृष्टि से ही नहीं, ऐतिहासिक दृष्टि से भी यह पुस्तक महत्वपूर्ण है और आरम्भ से अन्त तक सरल सुबोध भाषा में लिखी गयी है। इसके छपने के पहले भाई चन्द्रगुप्त जी विद्यालंकार ने इसे एक बार देख लिया था जो स्वयं बड़े सिद्धहस्त लेखक तथा सुयोग्य सम्पादक रह चुके हैं।

मेरा एक परामर्श और भी है इस पुस्तक के आरम्भ में बहन उर्मिलाजी के विषय में कुछ संस्मरण और शामिल कर लेने चाहिएँ, जिससे वह सूक्ष्म रूप से उस स्मृति ग्रन्थ का रूप धारण कर ले जो प्रत्येक नवयुवक तथा नवयुवती के पढ़ने योग्य हो।

—बनारसी दास चतुर्वेदी

प्रारम्भिक शब्द

हमारे जीवन में घटनाएँ होती हैं और चली जाती हैं, और तो कोई उन्हें देखता ही नहीं, पर हम स्वयं भी उन्हें नहीं देखते, क्योंकि हमें देखने की फ़ुर्सत नहीं होती, और हमारा ध्यान अनेक बाहरी घटनाओं में व्याकीर्ण रहता है। परन्तु जब मैं पिछले साल जेल की कोठरी में अकेली पड़ी हुई थी, जहाँ मेरा कोई साथी न था, तो उस समय मेरे पास सिवाय इसके कि मैं अपने जीवन की घटनाओं को देखूँ और उन पर विचार करूँ, और कोई काम ही न था। इस प्रकार इस पुस्तक की सामग्री जेल-जीवन में ही संचित हो गयी जिसे बाहर आ कर मैंने पुस्तकाकार दे डाला।

बाहर आने पर भी पुस्तक शीघ्र ही प्रकाशित न हो सकी। मुझे जेल में ही बुख़ार रहने लगा था और बाहर आ कर भी दो मास तक वह बना रहा। उसके बाद जब मैंने लाहौर से 'जन्मभूमि' नामक दैनिक पत्र का प्रकाशन किया, उसी में कुछ दिन तक मेरा जेल-जीवन का वृत्तान्त छपने लगा। उसे कई बन्धुओं ने पसन्द किया। 'जन्मभूमि' से उद्धृत कर कलकत्ते के दैनिक पत्र 'विश्वमित्र' ने भी जब मेरे जेल वृत्तान्त को छापा तो मेरा उत्साह बढ़ने लगा और मुझे यह ख़याल आया कि यदि इस वृत्तान्त को पुस्तकाकार छाप दिया जाय तो वह पढ़ने वालों के समय का दुरुपयोग न होगा।'जन्म-भूमि' पत्र के बन्द हो जाने से उस में यह वृत्तान्त प्रकाशित न हो सका, परन्तु मुझे प्रसन्नता है कि आज मैं एक पुस्तक के रूप में अपनी बहन और भाइयों की सेवा में उसे प्रस्तुत कर रही हूँ।

पूज्या माता कस्तूरी बाई जी के दर्शन मुझे मेरठ में हुए थे, और तभी से मुझे उनके चरणों में विशेष श्रद्धा हो गयी थी। मैं उनकी अत्यन्त कृतज्ञ हूँ कि उन्होंने कृपापूर्वक इस पुस्तक की प्रस्तावना लिखना स्वीकार किया।

श्रद्धेय जमनालालजी बजाज को मैंने यह पुस्तक समर्पित की है जो कि उचित ही था। लगभग चार साल हुए मैं देहरादून कन्या गुरुकुल में थी। वहाँ पर सौभाग्यवश वे पधारे और उन्होंने अपना बहुत-सा अमूल्य समय मुझे खादी का महत्व समझाने में लगाया था। उस समय तो मैं अपनी हार मानने को तैयार न हुई, परन्तु उनका लगाया बीज मेरे हृदय में अंकुरित हुए बिना न रहा। वस्तुतः श्रीयुत बजाज जी के द्वारा ही मुझे सब से प्रथम इस ओर प्रेरणा हुई थी।

इस पुस्तक के कतिपय भागों की द्वितीयावृत्ति मेरे भाई स्नातक चन्द्रगुप्त जी विद्यालंकार ने करने की कृपा की है, उसके लिए मैं उनकी कृतज्ञ हूँ।

—उर्मिला शास्त्री

मेरठ
२५.११.१९३१

कारागार

कारागार
पाप पुण्य का एकाकार,
स्वर्ग नरक का अनुपम द्वार।
संसार के पापियों का, आततताइयों का स्थान,
विश्व के पुनीत पुण्यात्माओं का निवास–
विरोधाभास की अनुपम पहेली
जहाँ गीता के प्रवर्त्तक कृष्ण का जन्म हुआ
जहाँ गीता के भाष्यकार तिलक ने तप किया
जहाँ गैलीलियो[1] ने सत्य की पूजा की
जहाँ जॉन बनियन ने विश्वविख्यात ग्रन्थ[2] लिखा
जहाँ धर्म गुरु[3] बह ने अपना जीवन बिताया

---

1. गैलीलियो यूरोप का प्रसिद्ध नक्षत्र-विज्ञान-वेत्ता था, जिसने सबसे पहले आकाश के ग्रहों-उपग्रहों को दूरवीक्षण यन्त्र से देखा था। उसके विचार बाइबल के प्रतिकूल थे, इसलिए रोम के पोप ने उसे बुढ़ापे की अवस्था में जेल में डलवा दिया।

2. जॉन बनियन नामक लेखक ने अपनी जगत प्रसिद्ध पुस्तक "The Pilgrim's Progress" जेल में लिखी थी।

3. फ़ारस के बहाई धर्म के आचार्य 'बहा' को फ़ारस की सरकार ने लगभग सारे जीवन जेल में ही रखा।

जो गाँधी की पुण्य गन्ध से सुगन्धित हो गया
वह कारागार! पुण्यागार!!

मनुष्य समाज जिन पापियों के दुराचार पर लज्जित होता है उन्हें वह छिपाने के लिए कारागार में बन्द कर देता है; पर वह जिन महात्माओं के पुण्य तेज के कारण स्वयं अपने ऊपर लज्जित होता है, उन्हें भी जेल में छिपा देता है।

वह पापियों के पाप को नहीं सह सकता
वह पुण्यात्माओं के पुण्य-तेज को भी नहीं सह सकता,
यह अद्‌भुत विडम्बना है।
मनुष्य की जन्म-सिद्ध स्वाधीनता का निषेध कारागार है
मनुष्य की स्वाधीनता का साधन भी कारागार है
यह एक अजीब पहेली है
सरकार का क़िला कारागार है और–
काँग्रेस का गढ़ भी कारागार है
शत्रु मित्र दोनों का एकाकार!
स्वाधीनता छीनने को सत्याग्रहियों को
कारागार में डाला जाता है।
स्वाधीनता के दर्शन सत्याग्रहियों को
कारागार में ही होते हैं,
कितना विचित्र विरोध है।
जेल बन्धन का रूप है और मनुष्य का जीवन भी बन्धन है,
इसलिए जीवन को बन्धन रूप दिखा कर
जेल चरम मुक्ति का मार्ग खोलता है।
हथकड़ी जेल का श्रृंगार है
बड़ी जेल का उपहार है
काल-कोठरी जेल की बहार है।
स्वाधीनता दीक्षा की विद्याभूमि,

सत्य के पुजारियों का मन्दिर,
स्वराज्य यात्रियों का तीर्थस्थान,
अध्यात्म-साधना का तपोवन,
हे कारागार! हे पुण्यागार!!
तुम्हारी धूल के स्पर्श से यह जघन्य जीवन धन्य है,
तुम्हें प्रणाम!
बारम्बार प्रणाम!!

अनुक्रम

1

जेल जाने से पहले

जुलाई सन १६३० की १६ तारीख़ थी, मैं अपना सामान कश्मीर जाने के लिए तैयार कर रही थी। उन दिनों मेरठ की बहनें बड़ी संख्या में सत्याग्रह-संग्राम में भाग ले रही थीं। उनके साथ लगभग चार मास तक अनवरत काम करने के बाद दो महीने का अवकाश मिला था। मन में बहुत उमंगें थीं। कश्मीर के प्राकृतिक दृश्य अभी से आँखों के आगे घूमने लगे थे। यहीं से अपना प्रोग्राम निश्चित कर रही थी कि अचानक सड़क पर से आवाज़ आयी – "पं. प्यारेलाल शर्मा गिरफ़्तार हो गये।"

शर्माजी मेरठ के एक माननीय प्रसिद्ध नेता हैं। मेरे दिल में खलबली मच गयी – अब क्या करना चाहिए? एक तरफ़ बहन-भाइयों से मिलने का चाव, शीतल-मन्द समीर का सेवन, और दूसरी तरफ़ कड़ी धूप और मेहनत का प्रश्न था और उसके बाद–जेल के लौहद्वार का दर्शन। देवासुर संग्राम छिड़ गया। कुछ तै न कर सकी। इसी बीच में प्रोफ़ेसरजी भीतर आये और कहने लगे, "उर्मिला क्या, निश्चय किया है? अच्छी तरह सोच लो–एक ओर कर्त्तव्य, तो दूसरी ओर सुख तथा विश्राम है, बताओ दोनों में किसे पसन्द करती हो?" इस प्रश्न ने हृदय में बल दिया, दैवी भावों ने सुख की अभिलाषा पर विजय पायी और मैंने अपना कर्त्तव्य निश्चित कर लिया।

दूसरे दिन शाम के लगभग चार बजे होंगे, मैं अपने कमरे में लेटी हुई थी। प्रोफ़ेसरजी पास ही बैठे हुए एक समाचार-पत्र पढ़ रहे थे। अचानक मैंने कहा–"चलो, आज एक साथ फ़ोटो खिचवायें।" प्रोफ़ेसरजी ने कौतूहल-भरी

दृष्टि से मेरी ओर देख कर गम्भीरता से उत्तर दिया—''ज़रूर, अभी चलने का निश्चय हो, तो सदर में मि. महमूद – एक प्रसिद्ध फ़ोटोग्राफ़र के पास चलें।''

मैं – ''फ़ोटोग्राफ़र से समय माँगिए।''

नौकर को भेज कर समय पूछा गया। उत्तर मिला—''अभी आ जाइए।''

मैं तैयार हो गयी। टाँगे पर बैठते ही मैंने देखा, शान्ता चली आ रही हैं। शान्ता महिला-सत्याग्रह-समिति की एक सदस्या तथा मेरी मित्र थीं। उनके हाथ में विलायती वस्तुओं के बहिष्कार सम्बन्धी कुछ नोटिस थे। वे अपना कार्य समाप्त करके, मुझसे मिलने आ रही थीं।

आते ही उन्होंने पूछा—''कहाँ को तैयार हो?''

मैंने हँसते-हँसते उत्तर दिया—''जहन्नुम को, चलती हो?''

शान्ता मुस्करा दीं और मेरे साथ टाँगे में बैठ गयीं।

मिस्टर महमूद पहले ही प्रतीक्षा में थे, तीन फ़ोटो लिये गये। लौटते हुए सदर की कोतवाली के पास पुलिस से भरी दो लॉरियाँ दिखाई दीं। इनके आगे डी.एस. पी. की मोटर थी। प्रोफ़ेसरजी ने कहा—''मालूम होता है कि सदर की शराब की दुकानों पर स्वयंसेवक गिरफ्तार किये जायेंगे।'' लारियाँ बाज़ार में चली गयीं। प्रोफ़ेसरजी ने गम्भीरता से कहा—''उर्मिला, कल तुम्हारी भी बारी है।''

मैंने पूछा, ''आपको कैसे मालूम?''

उन्होंने उत्तर दिया— ''मेरा दिल कह रहा है।''

मैंने हँसते हुए कहा—''आपके दिल की क्या बात। वह तो कुछ ही कहने लगता है।''

आज बर्फ़ख़ाने के मैदान में शर्माजी के जेल जाने के उपलक्ष्य में उन्हें बधाई दी जा रही थी। दिल कह रहा था, आज तुम भी दिल खोल कर बधाई दे लो, शायद आज ही अन्तिम मौक़ा है।

सभापति क़ाज़ी नज़ीमुद्दीन के पास जा कर मैंने कहा – ''क़ाज़ीजी, मुझे समय चाहिए, शायद मेरा यह आख़िरी मौक़ा होगा।''

क़ाज़ीजी ने एक बार मेरी ओर देखा और कहा—''अच्छी बात है, जितना चाहे समय लो।''

मेरी बारी आयी। मैं सभा मंच पर खड़ी हो गयी। जनता ने महात्मा गाँधी की जय की ध्वनि से मैदान कँपा दिया। मैंने अपने हार्दिक भाव बिखेर दिये। मैंने कहा—"कौन जानता है आने वाला चमकता सूर्य किस-किस की सुनहरी बेड़ियों को अपने साथ लायेगा।" ये शब्द सचमुच अपने सम्बन्ध में मेरी भविष्यवाणी सिद्ध हुए।

घड़ी ने ज्योंही टन करके एक बजाया, मेरी नींद खुल गयी।

मैंने देखा, प्रोफ़ेसरजी उठ कर बैठे हुए हैं, और मेरा सेवक गोवर्धन पास खड़ा है। मैंने पूछा—"क्या बात है, अभी तो रात का एक ही बजा होगा, आप उठ क्यों बैठे?"

प्रोफ़ेसरजी ने कहा—"इस घर में अब तुम चन्द घण्टों तक ही और रह सकती हो, उर्मिला!"

मैं उठ बैठी। मुझे कुछ समझ न आया। मैंने फिर अपने प्रश्न को दोहराया।

उन्होंने कहा—"प्रातःकाल ५ बजे तुम्हें लेने के लिए पुलिस आयेगी।"

मैंने अपना सामान ठीक करने के ख़याल से कहा—"अच्छा चलो, नीचे के कमरे में चलें।"

मैंने अपना साथ जाने वाला सामान अलग रख दिया। प्रोफ़ेसरजी ने कहा—"तुम सो जाओ, सामान तैयार हो जायेगा।"

लगभग सवा चार बजे होंगे कि मुझे प्रोफ़ेसरजी ने जगा कर कहा—"अब तैयार हो जाओ।"

मैंने स्नानादि करके कपड़े पहन लिये। ठीक ५ बजे एक लॉरी आयी और मेरे घर से कुछ दूर पर आड़ में खड़ी हो गयी। इस लॉरी में पुलिस के चार-पाँच सिपाही और पुलिस सब-इन्सपेक्टर था। एक मोटर मेरे दरवाज़े पर आ कर हॉर्न करने लगी। उस मोटर में केवल डी. एस. पी. और एक ड्राइवर ही थे। पास के घरों से कुछ स्त्री-पुरुष भी आ गये। 'महात्मा गाँधी की जय' कहते हुए मैं मोटर में बैठ गयी। मुझे जेल तक पहुँचाने के लिए प्रोफ़ेसरजी भी साथ ही चले। लोगों ने मुझे फूल उपहार में दिये, और मैंने चिरकाल के लिए उनसे नमस्कार कह कर विदा ली। कुछ क्षणों के बाद मोटर अब्दुल्लापुर के पास मेरठ डिस्ट्रिक्ट जेल के द्वार पर आ कर रुक गयी। साथ ही वह लॉरी भी आ पहुँची। डी. एस. पी. ने

कहा—"क़ाज़ी साहब भी लाये जा रहे हैं।" मैं उनसे मिलने के लिए दरवाज़े पर रुक गयी। क़ाज़ीजी भी एक लॉरी में सिपाहियों के साथ बैठे नज़र आये। प्रोफ़ेसरजी से विदा ले हम दोनों जेल द्वार के भीतर चले गये। दरवाज़ा बन्द हो गया, और मैं चिरकाल के लिए बाहर की दुनिया से जुदा कर दी गयी। मेरी तलाशी ली गयी। मेरे बिस्तर से तीन पुस्तकें, जिनमें से दो 'कल्याण' के विशेषांक थे, और एक साधारण कहानियों की पुस्तक थी, ले ली गयीं। मैं अपने साथ एक स्प्रिंगदार चरखा भी ले गयी थी, पर वह भी जेलर ने अपने पास रखवा लिया। घर से चलते हुए प्रोफ़ेसरजी ने मुझे एक पत्र दिया था, जिसे मैं शीघ्रता में ठीक-ठीक पढ़ न सकी थी, पढ़ने के लिए तथा अपने पास रखने के लिए मैं उसे अपने पर्स में डाल लायी थी, जेलर ने कहा—"यह पत्र मुझे दे दीजिए।"

मैंने कहा—"यह मेरे पति का पत्र है, यह मैं आपको नहीं दे सकती।"

जेलर—"फिर अगर आप इसे पढ़ चुकी हैं, तो इसे फाड़ डालें।"

मैंने उसी समय अपना प्यारा पत्र टुकड़े-टुकड़े कर दिया और भीतर अपने वॉर्ड की ओर चल दी।

2

जेल में पहला दिन

ज़िला जेलों में महिला-वॉर्ड बहुत छोटा-सा होता है, क्योंकि मुक़दमा हो जाने पर छः मास या उससे अधिक दण्ड वाली स्त्री सेण्ट्रल जेल में भेज दी जाती है। मेरठ ज़िला जेल में दीवार के भीतर एक कोने में एक और छोटी दीवार से घिरा हुआ महिला-वॉर्ड बना है। इस वॉर्ड का एक ही द्वार है, जो लोहे के मोटे तख़्ते से बना हुआ है। इस पर हर समय ताले पड़े रहते हैं, एक बाहर से बन्द किया जाता है और दूसरे को लेडी वॉर्डर भीतर से बन्द कर लेती हैं। बाहर की ताली दफ़्तर में और भीतर की ताली लेडी-वॉर्डर के पास रहती है। उसी द्वार के पास ला कर मुझे खड़ा कर दिया गया। मेरे साथ हेड वॉर्डर और मेरा सामान उठाये हुए एक क़ैदी नम्बरदार था। वॉर्डर ने बाहर से द्वार का ताला खोला और द्वार खटखटाया, तब भीतर से भी ताला खोला गया। द्वार खुल गया। वॉर्डर ने कहा—"चलिए, यहीं आपको रहना है।" मैं बिना उत्तर दिये चुपचाप भीतर चली गयी। मेरे भीतर होते ही बाहर का ताला बन्द कर दिया गया और उसी समय लेडी वॉर्डर ने भीतर का ताला भी बन्द कर दिया।

जमादारिन एक बड़ी आयु की ईसाई स्त्री थी, जिसका जन्म ब्राह्मण वंश में हुआ था। मुझसे कहा गया—"यह स्त्री पैदाइश से ब्राह्मण है, आप चाहें तो इससे खाने में मदद ले सकती हैं।"

द्वार के सामने एक लम्बी बैरक थी। उसी के द्वार पर दो छोटी उम्र की क़ैदिनें बैठी हुई मेरी ओर बड़ी उत्सुकता से देख रही थीं। उनके बाल खुले हुए थे तथा कपड़े फटे हुए और बहुत मैले थे।

जमादारिन मुझे उसी बैरक के भीतर ले गयी। बैरक में 17 लम्बी-लम्बी मिट्टी की चौकियाँ बनी हुई थीं, उन्हीं में से एक चौकी पर मेरा बिस्तर भी रख दिया गया। यही मेरा घर था।

मैंने बैरक के अन्दर घूम कर देखा। उसमें एक कोने में पाख़ाना भीतर ही बना था। मुझे इसी बैरक में सोना भी था, बड़ी कठिनता थी, पर क्या करती। पाखाने से छः चौकियाँ छोड़ कर एक कोने में अपना विस्तर बिछा ही लिया।

बैरक में छः बड़े-बड़े द्वार थे, जिनमें से एक को छोड़ कर सब पर सात-सात लोहे की मोटी छड़ें लगी थीं। ये सदा बन्द रहते थे, केवल एक द्वार जो लोहे की छड़ों द्वारा ही बनाया गया था, खुला रहता था। यह द्वार गर्मी-सर्दी दोनों ही समय के लिए दुःखदायी होते हैं। गर्मी में लुएँ, आँधी, धूप भीतर आ कर क़ैदियों के शरीरों को अकड़ा देती है। पर इन द्वारों से जेल अधिकारियों को सुविधा होती है। बन्द क़ैदी भीतर क्या कर रहा है, यह बाहर से प्रति क्षण दिखाई दे सकता है। अस्तु—मैं अपने बिस्तर को फैला कर बैठ गयी।

सहसा 'भारत माता की जय' के मधुर घोष से जेल गूँज उठी। मैं चौंक पड़ी। जेल में यह मधुर ध्वनि! पर मुझे समझने में देर नहीं लगी—पास की पुरुषों की बैरकों में जो राजनैतिक क़ैदी बन्द थे, उन्होंने क़ाज़ी साहब के पहुँचते ही स्वागतार्थ हर्षमय जय घोष किया था। मेरे दिल में आया—'क़ाज़ी साहब अपने साथियों में जा मिले हैं। उनका हर्ष और प्रेम से जयनाद द्वारा स्वागत सैकड़ों कण्ठों ने किया है, पर मेरा स्वागत? मेरा स्वागत केवल मूक-वायु ने हलकी-सी सर-सर ध्वनि करके ही समाप्त कर दिया।'

वहाँ मेरा कोई साथी न था।

हाँ, मेरी बैरक में दो स्त्रियाँ और भी रहती थीं। एक तो घर से भाग कर आयी थी, दूसरी को धर्म-परिवर्तन करने के कारण झगड़ा हो जाने से जेल भुगतनी पड़ रही थी।

वह एक ब्राह्मण की लड़की थी। इसके उत्पन्न होने के कुछ समय बाद उसके पिता ने मुस्लिम धर्म स्वीकार कर लिया था। इसीलिए बड़े होने पर एक मुस्लिम पुरुष से उसका विवाह कर दिया गया था, जो इसे बहुत मारा-पीटा करता था। इस तरह तंग आ कर उसने एक हिन्दू से शादी कर ली जहाँ उसे शुद्ध भी किया

गया, और आपस के हिन्दू-मुस्लिम झगड़े में उस स्त्री को छः मास का दण्ड मिला गया। वह स्त्री कोई उत्तम संस्कारों की न थी।

दोनों स्त्रियाँ धीरे-धीरे आयीं। उनमें से एक ने मुझसे पूछा—"तुम किस जुरम में आयी हो।"

मैंने मुस्करा कर कहा—"माँ को प्यार करने का जुर्म किया है।" दोनों स्त्रियाँ एक-दूसरी का मुँह देखने लगीं। उन्हें मेरी बात समझ नहीं आयी

कुछ देर में मुझे मूँज की बनी हुई एक चटाई और एक काला कम्बल दिया गया। चटाई नीचे बिछाने के लिए और कम्बल ऊपर ओढ़ने के लिए था। अभी एक घण्टा भी न बीता था जब द्वार खड़खड़ाया जाने लगा, जमादारिन भागी। ताला खोला गया। द्वार खुला तो जेलर और जेल सुपरिण्टेण्डेट साहब भीतर आते दिखायी दिये। मेरे लिए एक छोटी-सी छः सीटोंवाली बैरक ख़ाली करवायी गयी, उस बैरक की हालत पहली बैरक से कहीं अधिक बुरी थी। अतः मैंने वहाँ रहना स्वीकार नहीं किया। मेरे मना करने का एक और भी कारण था, मुझे 'ए' क्लास मिलने के कारण अकेले रखने का प्रबन्ध किया गया था। वैसे तो मेरे साथ की राजनैतिक क़ैदी कोई बहन वहाँ थी ही नहीं, और इख़लाकी क़ैदियों को भी मुझसे अलग रखने का प्रबन्ध किया जा रहा था। अस्तु, उसी लम्बी बैंरक में ही मेरा निवास-स्थान माना गया। मुझे जेल हस्पताल से एक लोहे का जालीदार पलँग दिलवा दिया गया। कुछ फल और एक पाव दूध प्रातः नाश्ते के लिए मुझे दिया गया और द्वार बन्द हो गया।

भूख तो लग ही रही थी, मैंने खाने के लिए सन्तरा उठाया। खोलते ही उसमें एक विचित्र चीज़ के दर्शन हुए, वह था एक छोटा-सा पत्र। पत्र का मज़मून यह था—

बहन जी,

बन्दे!

हम सब लोगों की ओर से आपको जेल आने के उपलक्ष में बधाई हो। जिस समय आप मुलाक़ात के लिए अपने वॉर्ड से बाहर जायें, हमारे वॉर्ड के द्वार की ओर देख लें, हम सींकचों में से ही आपको प्रणाम करना चाहते हैं।

हम हैं,

आपके भाई,
जेल के क़ैदी।

थोड़ी देर में मेरे वॉर्ड का द्वार फिर खुला। एक वॉर्डर एक क़ैदी के सिर पर कोई चीज़ लाता हुआ दिखाई दिया। वह था गद्दा। जेल द्वारा मुझे एक गद्दा भी बिछाने को मिला, पर उस गद्दे और काँटे के बिछौने में कुछ अन्तर न था। मामूली कपड़े के अन्दर गाय-भैंसों को खिलाये जाने वाला सूखा भूसा भरा हुआ था। मैंने उसे बिछाने की व्यर्थ चेष्टा की, कभी वह सब एक तरफ़ हो जाता और कभी दूसरी ओर पहुँच जाता। मैं हैरान थी, इसका क्या इस्तेमाल किया जाता होगा। जैसे-तैसे उसे लोहे के पलँग पर नीचे मूँज की चटाई बिछा कर उसके ऊपर यह गद्दा बिछा दिया। मैंने चाहा कि देखूँ, इस पर कैसे सोया जाता है। ज़रूर यह गद्दा जेल हस्पताल से दिलवाया गया होगा और रोगी ऐसे ही गद्दों पर सुलाये जाते होंगे, मैं भी तो देखूँ।

मैं गद्दे पर लेट गयी। आह! उन रोगियों की क्या दुर्दशा होती होगी। मैं गद्दे पर पूरा एक मिनट भी न लेट सकी। पैने-पैने तिनकों ने कपड़े के दबते ही अपने सिर बाहर कर लिये, हज़ार जिह्वाओं द्वारा डंक मारने के लिए गद्दे ने शेषनाग का रूप धारण कर लिया।

मैं उठ बैठी। गद्दा वापस कर दिया। ख़ाली खाट पर भी बिस्तर बिछाना कठिन था। खाट लोहे की बनी हुई थी, और उसमें भी बड़े-बड़े छेद-से बन रहे थे, जिससे बिस्तर के दबते ही जगह-जगह गड्ढे पड़ जाते थे। ख़ैर, मैंने मिट्टी की चौकी पर बिस्तर बिछाना ही पसन्द किया।

रात को नींद ठीक से न आयी थी, वैसे भी काम करते हुए थकावट प्रायः बनी ही रहती थी। ख़याल आया कि अब आराम करने के दिन आये हैं। सरकार ने इसीलिए बुला लिया है। मैं सोने की चेष्टा करने, लगी पर धूप निकल आयी थी, जुलाई का महीना था, गर्मी बहुत अनुभव होने लगी।

धूप रोकने का कोई (किवाड़ आदि) साधन नहीं था। मेरा जन्मस्थान इस पृथ्वी के स्वर्ग, कश्मीर में हुआ है। इस कारण गर्मी के दिनों में हर साल कश्मीर रहने का मुझे अभ्यास था। यह मेरी पहली गर्मियाँ थीं, जो मैंने मैदान में काटीं और वह भी जेल में, जहाँ गर्मी के साथ मच्छरों का भी अखण्ड राज्य था। ख़ैर मैंने सोने की कोशिश की; परन्तु दस बजे होंगे, वॉर्ड का द्वार खुला, एक जमादार ने आ कर सूचना दी कि प्रोफ़ेसरजी तुमसे मिलने आये है। मैं उठ कर वॉर्ड से बाहर आयी, द्वार से बाहर होते ही एक तरफ़ से आवाज़ आयी, 'बहनजी, वन्दे,भारत माता की जय।' मैंने चौंक कर देखा, पर कुछ स्पष्ट न देख सकी।

हाँ, इतना अन्दाज़ा हो गया कि मेरे भाई कहीं सींकचों में से मेरा स्वागत कर रहे हैं।

जेल के दफ़्तर में प्रोफ़ेसरजी एक कुर्सी पर बैठे हुए मेरी प्रतीक्षा कर रहे थे, वहीं मैं भी जा कर पास की एक कुर्सी पर बैठ गयी। प्रोफ़ेसरजी ने कहा—"शहर में हड़ताल हो गयी है। कॉलेज को बन्द करवाया जा रहा है, कई स्थानों पर हड़ताल करवाने के लिए बहनें पिकेटिंग कर रही हैं।" यह सुन मेरा दिल उछलने लगा—काश! मैं भी उनका साथ दे सकती।

बीस मिनट बीतते देर न लगी, जेलर ने कहा— "आपका समय समाप्त हो गया।" मैं उठ खड़ी हुई प्रोफ़ेसरजी को नमस्कार करके अपने वॉर्ड की ओर लौट पड़ी।

इस बार मुझे बारह नम्बर वॉर्ड दूर से दिखायी दिया, उसी वॉर्ड में परिचित भाई राजनैतिक क़ैदी बन्द थे, वह इतने दूर थे कि मैं उन्हें पहचान भी नहीं सकी। हाँ, 'बहनजी, वन्दे' के शब्द सुनाई देने लगे। मेरी इच्छा हुई, इन लोगों से कुछ बात करूँ, पर मैं 'क़ैदी' थी, बात करना मेरे अधिकार में न था। मजबूर हो कर मैं वॉर्ड के भीतर चली गयी।

इस के बाद वही मेरा वॉर्ड और वही मैं....द्वार बन्द हो गया। मैं बैरक में आ कर चटाई पर बैठ गयी। तरह-तरह की पिछली घटनाएँ रह-रह कर आँखों के आगे नाचने लगीं। प्रोफ़ेसरजी के यह शब्द 'अच्छा उर्मिला नमस्ते' कानों में गूँजने लगे। मैं सोचने लगी। अभी तो पहला ही दिन है। कहा करते थे, हम ग़ुलाम हैं, पर वास्तव में ग़ुलामी क्या चीज़ है, उसका अनुभव अब होने लगा। बन्द पक्षी पिंजरों से बाहर उड़ कर जाना चाहते हैं। पक्षियों की याद आते ही मेरी नज़र ख़ुद-ब-ख़ुद नीम के पेड़ की ओर चली गयी। यह पेड़ मेरे वॉर्ड में ही था। मुझे दिखाई दिया—उस पर अनेक पक्षी बैठते थे और जब चाहते थे उड़ जाते थे।

मैं अपने ध्यान में लगी थी, मुझे यह भी पता नहीं लगा कि वॉर्ड का द्वार कब खुला। हाँ, मैंने इतना देखा—एक थाली में खाना परस कर लाया गया है। खाना मेरे घर से आया था। इसलिए जेल के खाने का अनुभव उस समय मैं न कर सकी। दोपहर में कुछ वर्षा-सी होने लगी। मैं बैरक में चली गयी और दोपहर का वक़्त नींद में ही व्यतीत कर दिया।

शाम के चार बजे होंगे कि वॉर्ड का द्वार खुला। सामने मैदान में आते-जाते क़ैदी दूर से दिखाई देने लगे। किसी के हाथ में, तो किसी के पाँवों में लोहे के

ज़ेवर चमकते नज़र आ रहे थे। अदालत से क़ैदी लोग अपने भाग्यों का निर्णय ले कर चले आ रहे थे। मैं उत्सुकता से देखने लगी। इतने में देखा कि सिर पर एक बड़ी-सी पीतल की परात रखे हुए एक क़ैदी हमारे वॉर्ड के द्वार पर आया। उसके साथी के हाथ में एक लोहे की बाल्टी थी, वे लोग क़ैदियों को रोटी बाँट रहे थे। लेडी वॉर्डर ने पुकारा—"चलो, रोटी ले लो!"

क़ैदिनें अपना-अपना लोहे का तसला और कटोरी ले कर आगे बढ़ीं। रोटी परसने वाले ने पाँच-पाँच रोटियाँ और एक-एक कड़छी दाल की सबको बाँट दी। मैं भी यह देखने के लिए कि इन लोगों को कैसा खाना दिया जाता है, बैरक से बाहर द्वार के निकट आयी, मैंने अधखुले द्वार में से बाहर अहाते की ओर देखा, पण्डित प्यारे लाल शर्मा, चौधरी बिजयपाल सिंह, जगदीशचन्द्र आदि मेरठ के राजनैतिक क़ैदी चले आ रहे हैं। मैं नहीं कह सकती कि मुझे उन लोगों के देखने से कितना हर्ष और आनन्द हुआ। ठीक उसी तरह जैसे किसी निर्धन को अत्यन्त धन-राशि के दर्शन प्राप्त हो जायें। पर यह मेरा हर्ष स्थायी न रह सका। जमादार ने शीघ्र ही द्वार बन्द कर दिया।

शाम को मेरे लिए जेल से खाना आया, खाना अपनी ओर से शायद यत्न से बनाया गया था, पर मैं कोशिश करके भी उसे न खा सकी। आटे में रेत थी जो दाँतों के नीचे आ कर शरीर भर में एक विचित्र झनझनाहट उत्पन्न करने लगी। मैंने खाना छोड़ दिया; लेडी वॉर्डर ने कहा—"खा लो बीबी, दुःख मनाने की कौन-सी बात है?"

वॉर्डर यह नहीं समझ रही थी कि यह खाना खाया ही नहीं जा रहा, क्योंकि इस में रेत है। ख़ैर, मैंने खाना दूसरी क़ैदिनों को बाँट दिया।

लगभग साढ़े छः बजे होंगे कि द्वार खुला। जेलर साहब दो वॉर्डरों के साथ भीतर आये। आपने कहा—"अब बन्द किये जाने का समय है। आप भीतर चली जायें।"

मैं—"अभी से!"

जेलर—"जी हाँ, अभी से!"

मैं भीतर चली गयी। बैरक का लोहे के सींकचों वाला द्वार बन्द कर दिया गया। इसको लोहे की मोटी ज़ंजीर द्वारा कस दिया गया, जिस पर दो मोटे-मोटे लोहे के ताले डाल दिये गये।

उसके बाद बाहर के हाते के द्वार को भी बाहर से बन्द कर दिया गया। वॉर्ड के भीतर एक बैरक में दो तालों के अन्दर हम तीन स्त्रियाँ प्रातः पाँच बजे

तक के लिए बन्द हो गयीं। मैंने देखा—सूर्य भगवान अब भी उसी तरह चमक रहे हैं, उनकी रश्मियाँ लालिमामयी ज्योति से संसार को अब भी मुग्ध कर रही थीं। मैं बैरक के अन्दर ज़रा-से स्थान में ही टहलने लगी। मुझे ख़याल आया कि शहर में यही समय जुलूस निकलने का है। मैं कल्पना करने लगी – शहर में बड़ा भारी जुलूस निकल रहा होगा। स्त्रियाँ, बच्चे, बड़े, बूढ़े सभी हर्ष से उसमें सहयोग दे रहे होंगे। दुकानदार उसका स्वागत कर रहे होंगे, अब मीटिंग होगी, विदेशी कपड़े की होली जलायी जायेगी। फिर ख़याल आया कि मैं तो अब इस सबसे वंचित हो गयी हूँ।

विचारधारा समाप्त हो गयी, पर अब भी आकाश पर लाली थो। अभी नींद का समय नहीं था। अन्दर टहलने के लिए जगह भी नहीं थी। मैं लेट गयी। लेटते ही मच्छरों ने अपने प्रेमपूर्ण मधुर गान से रात्रि में होने वाले काण्ड की सूचना अभी से दे दी। कोई मच्छर हाथ पर तो कोई पैर पर बैठ कर मेरा आतिथ्य करने लगा। मेरे दुर्भाग्य से हवा भी बन्द हो गयी थी। मारे गर्मी और मच्छरों के साक्षात नरक के दर्शन होने लगे। मैं कभी लेट जाती, और कभी बैठ जाती और कभी टहलने लगती। मेरी साथी क़ैदिनें मेरी इस क़वायद पर ध्यान न दे कर अपनी ग्रामीण भाषा में गाने लगीं। मुझे बड़ा आश्चर्य होने लगा, मेरी तो बुरी हालत हो रही थी, पर वे दोनों आनन्द से मिट्टी की खाटों पर पाँव फैला कर गा रही थीं। पर नींद उन लोगों को भी नहीं आ रही थी।

जैसे-तैसे रात का एक बजा। मैं बिस्तर पर लेट गयी, पर अधिक देर तक लेटी न रह सकी। मैं जेल में आज ही आयी थी। मच्छर मेरा स्वागत गान मुझे विशेष रूप से सुनाना चाह रहे थे, पर मैंने उनकी अवज्ञा करके सोने की कोशिश की थी, इस पर वे रूठ गये। अन्त में उनके काटने से मेरी नींद खुल गयी और फिर प्रातः तक नहीं आयी। ख़याल था कि थोड़ी देर में दिन निकल आयेगा। पर जेल के घण्टे की आवाज़ से मालूम हुआ कि अभी दो ही बजे हैं; मैंने मन्त्र-पाठ शुरू कर किया। बचपन से आज तक जो भी कोई मन्त्र और श्लोक पढ़े या याद किये थे, उन सभी की आवृत्ति कर डाली, परन्तु आश्चर्य कि यह मन्त्र पाठ समाप्त हो गया, मगर रात्रि अब भी शेष थी। अन्त में परमात्मा को दया आयी—क्रमशः शीतल मन्द समीर के झोंके आने लगे, और उन्होंने थपकियाँ दे कर मुझे सुलाना चाहा—पर सहसा द्वार खड़खड़ाया गया; आवाज़ आयी—'उठ जाओ....दरवाज़ा खुलता है।'

3

अदालत का स्वाँग

खटखटाहट सुन कर हम लोग उठ कर बैठ गयीं। तब जमादारिन के साथ दो जमादारों ने आ कर बैरक का द्वार खोल दिया। हमारी गिनती की गयी और वॉर्ड बन्द कर दिया गया। अब मुझे स्नान करने आदि के लिए आज्ञा मिली, और मैं परमात्मा का धन्यवाद करती हुई बैरक से बाहर निकली।

लगभग ग्यारह बजे होंगे, मुझे सूचना मिली कि प्रोफ़ेसरजी और दूसरे लोग मुझ से मिलने आये हैं। वॉर्ड का द्वार खुला। एक वॉर्डर के और लेडी वॉर्डर के साथ मैं दफ़्तर में पहुँची। मैंने देखा, प्रोफ़ेसरजी के साथ पं. रामस्वरूप शर्मा (जत्थेदार, हिन्दुस्तानी सेवा दल) भी आये हैं। मुझे बड़ी प्रसन्नता हुई। प्रोफ़ेसरजी ने पूछा—"कुछ तकलीफ़ तो नहीं?"

मैं—"नहीं जी।"

प्रोफ़ेसरजी—"आज तुम्हारा भी मुक़दमा होगा।"

मैं—"कहाँ? अदालत में..."

प्रोफ़ेसरजी—"नहीं जेल के भीतर।"

शर्माजी ने कहा—" लोग आपको देखना चाहते हैं।"

मैं इसका क्या उत्तर दे सकती थी....समय समाप्त हो गया। प्रोफ़ेसरजी चले गये, मैं फिर अपनी बैरक में आ गयी।

नया स्थान था, कोई परिचित-अपरिचित अच्छी सोसाइटी का साथ नहीं था। सिर्फ़ दो क़ैदिनें थीं। उनकी बहुत-सी बातों से तबीयत घबराने लगी। मैं बैरक से उठ कर बाहर एक पेड़ के नीचे कम्बल बिछा कर बैठ गयी। घर की याद,

मित्रों की स्नेहमयी बातें– रह-रह कर याद आने लगीं, तबीयत घबराने लगी; मैंने उनको भुलाने के ख़याल से सोने की चेष्टा की।

अर्धनिद्रित अवस्था में मेरे सामने एक चित्र-सा खिंच गया–शहर में जुलूस निकल रहा है, बड़ा भारी जुलूस है, बहुत-सी पताकाएँ जुलूस की सुन्दरता बढ़ा रही हैं। हज़ारों स्त्री-पुरुषों के झुण्ड उसमें आ-आ कर सम्मिलित हो रहे हैं। सब से आगे स्त्रियाँ गाती हुई जा रही हैं–

"बाग़ में सर-सर का झोंका, आशियाना ले गया।
क़ैद में हम को हमारा आबोदाना ले गया।।
गुल गुले गुलचीं का शिकवा, बुलबुले भारत न कर।
तुमको पिंजरे में तेरा यह चहचहाना ले गया।।
कौन कहता है ज़बरदस्ती से हम पकड़े गये।
जेल में ख़ुद हम को शौक़े-क़ैदख़ाना ले गया।"

मैंने भी उनके स्वर में मिला कर गाना शुरू किया–
"हम को पिंजरे में हमारा, चहचहाना ले गया।।"

अचानक लेडी वॉर्डर ने आवाज़ दी। मैं चौंक उठी। अरे यहाँ तो कहीं जुलूस नहीं, यह तो वही कम्बल है, जिस पर जेल के अन्दर लेटी हुई हूँ। मैंने अपने स्वप्न को सोचना शुरू किया, ठीक तो है हम जान-बूझ कर ही तो जेल आये हैं। दिल में ख़याल आया–अगर मैं ऐसा नहीं करती तो? तो आत्मा ने कहा तो बड़ा भारी पाप होता। तुमने अपनी माँ को प्यार किया। अगर यह गुनाह है तो दुनिया में पुण्य क्या हो सकता है? मैंने आत्माभिमान के साथ कहा; अगर इस इक्कीस साल की उम्र में कोई पुण्य किया है, तो वह यही है। मेरा चेहरा खिल उठा, दिल में उत्साह-भरी तरंगें उठने लगीं, जोश में मैंने गुनगुनाना शुरू किया–

"कौन कहता है ज़बरदस्ती से हम पकड़े गये।
क़ैद में ख़ुद हमको शौक़े क़ैदख़ाना ले गया।"

ज्यों-ज्यों मैं इसे गाने लगी, मेरा उत्साह बढ़ने लगा। जमादारिन ने फिर आवाज़ दी–"तुम्हारे मुक़दमे का वक़्त हो गया।"

मैंने ख़ुशी से कहा—"अच्छी बात है।"

जमादारिन—"तुम्हारे मुक़दमे का पता नहीं क्या नतीजा होगा।"

मैं—"सज़ा मिलेगी।"

जमादारिन—"कितनी?"

मैं—"मेरे काम को देख कर छः मास की तो देगा ही।"

जमादारिन—"ऐसा मत कहो बहन।"

जेल के मुख्य द्वार के ठीक ऊपर जेल का दफ़्तर है। यहीं मेरे भाग्य का फ़ैसला करने का प्रबन्ध किया गया था। मैं वॉर्ड से बाहर निकली, सींकचों में से सुनायी दिया—'भारत माता की जय,' मैंने भी बिना पहचाने हाथ जोड़ दिये और आगे चल पड़ी। द्वार पर बड़ी भीड़ थी, कड़कती हुई दुपहरी के ठीक तीन बजे खुले मैदान में स्त्री और बच्चों को देख कर मेरा दिल दुखने लगा, पर आनन्द भी हुआ। यह लोग मुझे से प्रेम रखते हैं। हाथ जोड़ कर सब को दूर ही से नमस्कार करती हुई मैं दफ़्तर की ओर चल दी।

ऊपर कमरे के ऐन बीच में एक बड़ी-सी मेज़ के सामने ज्वाइण्ट मैजिस्ट्रेट मि. कौगिल बैठे थे। पास दो-तीन क्लर्क मुक़दमों में सहायता देने के लिए थे। मेज़ के दोनों ओर की सीटें मुक़दमा देखने वालों से भरी हुई थीं। मेरे से पहले शर्माजी आदि का मुक़दमा हो रहा था। उनके समाप्त होते ही मेरी बुलाहट हुई। मेज़ के पास बैठने की मुझे कुर्सी दी गयी। मैंने बैठते हुए कहा कि मेरा मुक़दमा शुरू होने से पहले उन्हें बुला लेना ज़रूरी है जिन्होंने मेरा मुक़दमा सुनने के लिए अर्ज़ी दे रखी है।

बहुत-सी बहनें और भाई ऊपर आ गये। जगह कम होने के कारण कइयों को सीढ़ियों में ही खड़ा होना पड़ा। मुक़दमा शुरू होते ही मैंने कहा कि सारी कार्यवाही हिन्दी में ही होनी चाहिए। ऐसा ही हुआ। मुझे बताया गया कि तुमने १३ तारीख़ को टाउन हॉल में विद्यार्थियों की मीटिंग में उन लोगों को सम्बोधित करते हुए कहा था—'तुम लोग शराब की दुकान पर धरना दो, शराब की दुकान बन्द करवा देना तुम्हारा कर्त्तव्य है।' मुझ से पूछा गया 'क्या आप मंज़ूर करती हैं?"

मैंने कहा—"जी हाँ।"

फिर कहा गया यह काम क़ानून के ख़िलाफ़ किया गया है। आप पर पिकेटिंग आर्डिनेंस के मुताबिक़ मुक़दमा चलाया जाता है।

मैं–"अच्छी बात है।"

फिर पूछा गया–"आप गवाही चाहती हैं या स्वीकार करती हैं।"

मैंने कहा–"स्वीकार है।"

मेरी एक बहन ने मुझ से कहा–"अरे, यह क्या करती हो? ज़रा उनकी शक्ल तो देख लेने दो जिन्हें तुम्हारे ख़िलाफ़ गवाही देने के लिए यहाँ लाया गया है।"

मुक़दमे का नाटक तो समाप्त हो गया था। मैजिस्ट्रेट ने हुक्म सुनाते हुए कहा–"आप लीडर हैं, इसलिए आपको छः मास की सादा सज़ा दो जाती है, जो इस धारा के अनुसार ज़्यादा-से-ज़्यादा दी जा सकती है।"

मैंने मैजिस्ट्रेट को इस उपहार के लिए धन्यवाद दिया। मेरी बहनों ने मुझे फूलमालाएँ उपहार में दीं। मैं सबको नमस्कार करती हुई नीचे आ गयी, जेल के द्वार पर खड़ी जनता ने उत्सुकता से पूछा–"क्या मिला।"

मैंने उत्तर दिया–"कुल छः मास।" सबने आशीर्वादमय बधाई के वाक्य कहे और मैं भीतर आ गयी। मेरे लिए जेल का द्वार छः मास के लिए बन्द हो गया। जेल के भीतर के भाइयों ने, जिनका अभी मुक़दमा हुआ था, जयघोष द्वारा मुझे बधाई दी। और मैं अपनी बैरक में पहुँचा दी गयी। मेरे दिमाग़ में तरह-तरह की बातें चक्कर काटने लगीं। अभी दस मास भी नहीं हुए थे जब मेरा विवाह हुआ था। मेरे पूज्य पिता, भाई और बहन सुन्दर कश्मीर में हैं जहाँ मेरा सुनहला बचपन बीता है। चार बरस हुए मेरी प्यारी जननी को जग-माता ने सदा के लिए अपनी गोद में बुला लिया था, मेरी माँ मुझ से छिन गयी। फिर विवाह के बाद भाई-बहनों का भी बिछोह हो गया। यहाँ मेरठ में आ कर नये सिरे से नया संसार बसाया था। आज वह भी छूट गया। छः मास के लिए जेल की दीवारें मेरी मित्र होंगी, वायु मेरी बातों का मूक उत्तर दिया करेगी। पेड़ों पर बैठे पक्षी ही मेरे प्रश्नों को सुनेंगे। छः मास उफ़! बड़ा लम्बा समय है, पर साथ ही ख़याल आया–यह क्या सोच रही हूँ। यह तो मुझे प्रभु ने मुँह-माँगी मुराद दी है। मैं स्वयं ही तो आयी हूँ। मेरे इस कष्ट से सम्भवतः माँ के संकटों में कुछ कमी हो सकेगी। इस विचार ने पहले विचारों को बदल दिया। दूसरी क़ैदिनों ने पूछा–"क्यों बीबी, क्या फ़ैसला हुआ?"

मैं–"छः मास मिले हैं।" अब छः मास कहते दुख नहीं था, हर्ष था, आनन्द था। मैंने सुना कि मेरे साथ जितने भी और भाई पकड़े गये थे, उन सभी को छः मास का ही उपहार मिला है।

4

सज़ा के बाद

बीस जुलाई से मेरे छः मास शुरू होते थे। मैंने बैठे-बैठे हिसाब लगाया, आज 20 तारीख़ है। जनवरी में जा कर किस दिन मुझे इस स्थान को छोड़ कर अपने प्यारे मित्रों और सम्बन्धियों के दर्शन हो सकेंगे। बड़ी लम्बी कल्पना थी—जनवरी में मेरे छूटने की तारीख़ आयेगी। मेरे घरवाले उस तारीख़ की कितने चाव से प्रतीक्षा कर रहे होंगे। दिन निकलते ही सब-के-सब जेल से मुझे लिवा जाने की तैयारियों में लगेंगे, उस तैयारी में उन्हें कितना आनन्द मिलेगा। ठीक दस बजे मुझे बुलाया जायेगा, मैं पहले से ही तैयार हो जाऊँगी, जेल के दफ़्तर में मुझे बुला कर मुझे घर जाने की आज्ञा दी जायगी। मेरी आँखों के सामने उस दिन का पूरा दृश्य खिंच गया। मैं अपनी कल्पना द्वारा देखने लगी—वॉर्डर ने लोहे का बड़ा द्वार खोल दिया है और मैं उस द्वार से बाहर गयी हूँ। आहहः! मेरे सम्बन्धियों के चेहरों पर कितना उल्लास है, कितना आनन्द है। सभी बार-बार मुझ से मिल रहे हैं।

मैं अपनी कल्पना में डूबी हुई थी, सहसा ज़ोर से किवाड़ का ताला हिलाया गया। यह इशारा वॉर्ड के बाहर से द्वार खुलने पर भीतर वालों को सावधान करने के लिए हुआ करता है। मैं चौंक उठी, पर शीघ्र ही मैंने अपनी आँखें फिर बन्द कर लीं। मैं चाहती थी, वह दृश्य मेरी आँखों से लोप न हो। मुझे ऐसा प्रतीत होने लगा जैसे सत्य ही मेरी छूटने की तिथि आ गयी है। मुझे बुलाने के लिए द्वार खोल कर वॉर्डर आया है। वॉर्डर ने आवाज़ दी—"चलिए।"

मैंने आश्चर्य से उसकी ओर देखा। वॉर्डर ने फिर कहा—"चलिए, साहब बुलाते हैं।"

मैं—"मुझे! किसलिए?"

वॉर्डर—"आपका मुलाहिज़ा होगा।"

मेरा स्वप्न मिट गया। उफ़, आज तो उन महीनों का पहला ही दिन है? अभी से....मेरी तबीयत घबराने लगी, अभी तो इन्हीं दीवारों के भीतर, इन्हीं जमादारों की देख में पूरे छः मास व्यतीत करने हैं। मैं यही सोच रही थी कि वॉर्डर ने मेरे बहुत पास आ कर फिर कहा—"बहन जी, शीघ्र चलिए, नहीं तो...."

"नहीं तो क्या?" मैंने चौंक कर कहा।

वॉर्डर—"साहब जवाब तलब करेंगे।"

मैं उठी और वॉर्डर के साथ चल पड़ी। अपने द्वार के बाहर होते ही मैंने देखा, ठीक सामने आँगन मे एक कुर्सी पर जेल के सुपरिण्टेण्डेण्ट कर्नल अब्दुल रहमान बैठे हैं, उनके सामने दो लम्बी क़तारें सज़ा पाये हुए क़ैदियों की खड़ी हैं, जिनमें कई सत्याग्रही भी हैं। परन्तु उस वर्दी में जो 'सी क्लास' के क़ैदियों को मिलती है, किसी को दूर से पहचान लेना बड़ा कठिन था। सुपरिण्टेण्डेण्ट की कुर्सी के पीछे सरकारी पोशाक पहने जेल डॉक्टर और क्लर्क आदि खड़े थे। मुझे भी वहीं ले जा कर क़ैदियों के पास खड़ा कर दिया गया। मैंने देखा सत्याग्रही क़ैदी मुझे नमस्ते करना चाहते हैं। उनकी दृष्टि, उनकी मजबूरी स्पष्ट बता रही थी कि अगर वे मुँह से कुछ भी बोलेंगे तो उन पर कोड़े पड़ने लगेंगे। जेलर क्रूर दृष्टि से क़ैदियों की ओर घूर रहा था।

इसी समय सुपरिण्टेण्डेण्ट ने मुझसे पूछा—"क्या आप अच्छी तरह हैं?"

मैं—"जी हाँ।"

सुप.—"आपका ही नाम उर्मिला शास्त्री है?"

मैं—"जी हाँ।"

सुप.—"क्या आप अपील करना चाहती हैं?"

मैं—"नहीं।"

सुपरिण्टेण्डेण्ट ने गम्भीरतापूर्वक मेरी ओर देखते हुए कहा—"जमादारिन, इन्हें ले जाओ।"

बस, मेरा मुलाहिज़ा हो गया। मैं चली आयी और उसी वॉर्ड में, उसी बैरक में, अपनी चटाई पर आ कर बैठ गयी। सारी उदासी काफ़ूर हो गयी। मैं अब प्रसन्न थी। जमादारिन ने अपने आप ही दूसरी क़ैदिनों से कहना शुरू किया—"देखो, साहब ने इनसे अपील के लिए पूछा पर यह मना कर आयीं। अपील करतीं, तो साफ़ छूट जातीं।"

उन दोनों में से एक ने कहा—''अजी इनका क्या है, जब चाहेंगी छूट सकती हैं। इन पर तो गाँधी महाराज का हाथ है, वह इन्हें एकदम छुटा लेंगे।''

मैं—''कैसे? वह तो ख़ुद जेल में हैं।''

क़ैदिन —''अजी, कहने को जेल में हैं, उनको कौन बन्द कर सकता है। हमने तो सुना है—एक बार उन्हें सात तालों में बन्द किया गया, ताले पड़े ही रहे, और गाँधी महाराज अपनी शक्ति से जेल के बाहर आ गये।''

मैं—''अच्छा, यह तुम्हें सुनाया किसने?''

क़ैदिन—'वाह, तुम जानती हुई भी ऐसा कहती हो! सारा गाँव तो कहता है।''

मैंने हँस कर कहा—'हाँ, ऐसा ही होगा।''

मुझे इन लोगों के अन्धविश्वास को मिटाने की इच्छा नहीं हुई। हाँ, यह बात बार-बार मेरे मन में उठने लगी कि इन लोगों की बातें किसे सुनायें! मेरा ध्यान फिर से अपने मित्रों की ओर खिंचने लगा, दिल में एक दर्द होने लगा—आह, मैं अपने भावों को दूसरों तक नहीं पहुँचा सकती। ख़याल आया, पत्र लिखूँ, पर मेरे पास काग़ज़ तक न था! लिखने का साधन, फ़ाउण्टेन पेन तो मेरे साथ है, पर काग़ज़! वह अभी तक नहीं मिला। अब क्या करूँ? मन बहलाने के लिए मैं किताब ले कर पढ़ने लगी। इसी समय, फिर से द्वार पर खटका होने लगा, सब की दृष्टि उसी ओर खिंच गयी। द्वार खुला, सर पर चटाई और कम्बल रखे हुए, एक हाथ से तसला-कटोरी लिये और दूसरे से छोटे बच्चे को गोद में सँभाले हुए, क़ैदियों के वेश में एक स्त्री भीतर आती दिखाई दी। दोनों क़ैदिनों का कौतूहल बढ़ गया। क़ैदिन ने द्वार के भीतर आते ही सर की चटाई और कम्बल ज़मीन पर पटक दिया। लेडी वॉर्डर को सलाम करके वह सीधी बैरक में आ पहुँची। उसे देख कर मुझे आश्चर्य हुआ, क्योंकि उसके चेहरे पर दुःख का कोई भाव न था, कमज़ोर इतनी थी कि उसके चेहरे की एक-एक हड्डी निकल आयी थी, उसकी आँखों में रोहे पड़ गये थे, जिनसे पानी निकल रहा था, लेडी वॉर्डर उसे पहले से जानती थी। साल भर पहले वह इसी जेल में एक वर्ष की सज़ा पा कर फ़तहगढ़ सेण्ट्रल जेल भेज दी गयी थी, उसका नाम मुहम्मदी था। अब छोड़े जाने के लिए वापस मेरठ लायी गयी थी। उसने लेडी वॉर्डर से पूछा—''यह बीबी कौन हैं?''

लेडी वॉर्डर—''यह काँग्रेसवाली[1] हैं।''

---

1. जेल में राजनैतिक क़दी इसी नाम से बुलाये जाते हैं।

मुहम्मदी ने मुझ से कहा—"सलाम बीबी!"

लेडी वॉर्डर ने उन क़ैदिनों के हाल पूछने शुरू किये जो यहाँ से फ़तहगढ़ भेजी जा चुकी थीं। बहुत देर तक बातें होती रहीं मुझे भी फ़तेहगढ़ सेण्ट्रल जेल के हाल जानने की इच्छा थी, मैंने पूछा—"वहाँ तुम्हारे साथ कैसा सलूक़ होता था?"

मुहम्मदी—"बीबी, कुछ मत पूछो, ज़रा-सी बात पर मार पडने लगती थी; नम्बरदारिनें और बैरकदारिनें तो हमारा ख़ून ही पी जाती थीं।"

लेडी वॉर्डर ने ताने से कहा—"क्यों, सुख भी तो बहुत देती हैं।"

मुहम्मदी—"जिन्हें देती हैं, उन्हें ही देती हैं, मेरी तो रो-रो कर आँखें ही ख़राब हो गयी।"

मुझे बड़ा आश्चर्य हुआ। सुख जिन्हें देती हैं इससे क्या मतलब, मैंने पूछा—"जो रिश्वत देती होंगी, उन्हें तंग न करती होंगी।"

मुहम्मदी और लेडी वॉर्डर एक-दूसरे की ओर देख कर मुस्करायीं। मैं और भी चकरायी। मैंने फिर पूछा—"क्या बात है?"

मुहम्मदी—"जो लड़कियाँ ख़ूबसूरत होती हैं उन्हें आराम रहता है। उन्हें वह अपने पास से खिलाती हैं..."

इसके बाद जो-जो बातें उसने बतलायीं, उन्हें सुन कर मैं काँप उठी....हे भगवन!....मैं उन बातों को लिख भी नहीं सकती। मैं कह नहीं सकती कि उसकी बातें कहाँ तक ठीक थीं, पर उनकी कल्पना से ही दिल घबराने लगता है।

मैंने पूछा—"क्या लेडी जेलर इन बातों को नहीं जानतीं?"

मुहम्मदी—"सब जानती हैं।"

मैं—"फिर प्रबन्ध क्यों नहीं करती। यों तो बात-बात पर मार पड़े, तनहाई मिले और इधर ध्यान भी न दिया जाये।"

मुहम्मदी—"बीबी, रिश्वत दुनिया में सबसे बड़ी चीज़ है।"

मैं चुप हो गयी। इसके बाद मैं प्रश्न भी क्या करती। मुहम्मदी ने स्वयं ही कहना शुरू किया—"क़ैदिनें दूसरों के बच्चों को ज़िद से हौज़ में गिरा देती हैं, यहाँ तक कि एक बच्चा मर भी गया था, पर जिसने गिराया था, लेडी वॉर्डर उस पर मेहरबान थी; सबने यह कह कर छुट्टी पा ली, कि बच्चा ख़ुद ही गिर कर मर गया।"

इसी प्रकार बहुत देर तक वह अपनी कहानी कहती रही। इतने में द्वार पुनः खड़खड़ाया गया, लेडी वॉर्डर ने आवाज़ दी—"चलो, रोटी ले लो।"

जेल में राजनैतिक क़ैदी इसी नाम से बुलाये जाते हैं

5

जेल-जीवन की झलक

अब तक तो वहाँ दो ही स्त्रियाँ थीं, और दोनों भी पहली बार जेल आयी थीं, उनका स्वभाव पहचानने में मुझे कुछ विशेष कठिनता नहीं हुई थी; पर अब नयी आयी हुई स्त्री साल भर फ़तहगढ़ सेन्ट्रल जेल में रह कर अपराधों में निपुणता प्राप्त करके आयी थी। ऐसा प्रतीत होता था कि मानो उसे अपने क़ैदी होने का रंज ही न था। वह अपने दुख को भुला कर आमोद-प्रमोद में मस्त रहती थी। यों तो भूल जाने का स्वभाव मनुष्य को परमात्मा की ओर से दिया गया है। यदि मनुष्य अपने प्रत्येक कष्ट और मुसीबतें सदा याद रखता तो प्रत्येक मनुष्य हर समय आँसू बहाता ही नज़र आता।

हमारी वॉर्डर को ख़ुद भी नाच और गान का शौक़ था; वह ख़ुद तो इसमें हिस्सा नहीं लेती थी, पर दूसरी क़ैदिनों का नाच और गान होने लगा। नाचने और गाने के भी कई ढंग होते हैं। ऐसा अश्लील नाच और गान मुझे अपनी आयु में देखने और सुनने को नहीं मिला था। वैसे तो दुर्भाग्य से हमारे देश का कोई प्रान्त अश्लील गान गाने और सुनने से न बचा होगा। पर यह अश्लीलता अभी तक गाँवों के गान और नाचों में बहुत कम, यहाँ तक कि नहीं के बराबर ही पायी जाती है। यह गुण तो शहरों में ही अधिक पाये जाते हैं। मेरे पिता आर्यसमाजी विचारों के हैं, वह प्रत्येक बात और सिद्धान्त को पूरी तरह अमल में लाने और उसका संस्कार अपनी सन्तान पर डालने का प्रयत्न करते हैं, मेरी स्वर्गीय माताजी भी इस काम में उनकी पूरी सहयोगिनी थीं। मुझे याद है—हमें कभी किसी शादी में गाने के स्थान पर नहीं जाने दिया जाता था। यहाँ तक कि विवाह से पूर्व मैंने एक भी ड्रामा, थियेटर, अच्छा या बुरा नहीं देखा था। किसी तरह के नाचादि

के देखने का मौक़ा ही क्या मिलता? वैसे मैं नृत्य-गान के विरुद्ध नहीं, वे उच्च श्रेणी की कलाएँ हैं। प्राचीन काल में भारत में इनका अच्छा प्रचार था। और यहाँ तक कि नृत्य-गान का सम्बन्ध धार्मिक कार्यों में – विशेषकर भक्ति मार्ग से – था। पर जिस नृत्य-गान का मैं वर्णन कर रही हूँ, वह तो बहुत अश्लील और गन्दा था, कोई भी सभ्य व्यक्ति इसे देखना पसन्द नहीं कर सकता। ख़ैर, यह सब राग और नाच रोज़ होने लगे, और धीरे-धीरे उनके साथ लड़ाई-झगड़े का जन्म भी हो गया। अश्लीलता में जो क़सर रह गयी थी, वह यहाँ पूरी हो गयी अब उन क़ैदिनों का सारा दिन गाली बकने, लड़ने या गन्दे गाने में गुज़रने लगा। कभी-कभी रोना-धोना भी शुरू हो जाता था। लड़ाई का अन्त तो प्रायः ऊँचे स्वर से रोने ही में होता था। ख़ैर, जो कुछ भी हो, वह सब थीं तो एक ही स्वभाव की; पर मैं अकेली थी। एक रात तो उन्होंने ग़ज़ब ही कर दिया, अभी ताला बन्द ही हुआ था, एक स्त्री को शौक़ सवार हुआ। उसने कहा–"चलो, आज सुरमा बना कर लगायें।" उन्होंने सरसों का तेल, जो उन्हें सर पर लगाने को मिला था, ले कर जैसे-तैसे कालिख तैयार की; अब लड़ाई शुरू हुई किसी ने ज़्यादा लगा लिया, किसी को कम मिला, बस दोनों ने कमर बाँध कर युद्ध-क्षेत्र में पदार्पण किया। मेरी मुसीबत आ गयी, मैं भी उसी बैरक में रहती थी, मेरी बड़ी इच्छा हुई कि इन लोगों को शान्त करा दूँ, कहीं वॉर्डर ने पेश कर दिया तो मुफ़्त मारी जायेंगी; पर वहाँ तो दोनों ही एक-दूसरे को फाड़ खाने को तैयार हो रही थीं। रात को बारह बजे का घण्टा बजने लगा, तब तो मुझसे न रहा गया, मैंने उन लोगों को चुप रहने को कहा।

एक ने जबाब दिया, "तुम्हीं बता दो, मैंने क्या कहा है?"

दूसरी ने झट से कहा, "तो मैंने ही क्या कह दिया?"

मैं चुप हो गयी। मैं उनकी इस दलील का जबाब क्या देती। वह फिर उसी तरह लड़ने लगीं, मजबूर हो कर मुझे वॉर्डर को आवाज़ देनी पड़ी, किन्तु वहाँ और भी तामाशा हो गया। उन दोनों में से एक ने उठ कर स्वयं वॉर्डर को रो-रो कर बुलाना शुरू किया। ख़ैर, उनकी ख़ुशक़िस्मती से वॉर्डन ने सुना ही नहीं या रात में दरवाज़ा खोलने की परेशानी से बचने के लिए बोली ही नहीं। मैंने कहा–"देखो, वॉर्डर के आने पर मैं तुम दोनों की बात कह दूँगी. इससे अच्छा है चुप हो जाओ।" इस बात का असर हो गया और वह दोनों कहीं एक बजे जा कर सो गयीं।

वे लोग तो लड़-लड़ा कर बेफ़िकरी से सो गयीं, पर यहाँ नींद हराम हो गयी। सारी रात चिन्ता में ही व्यतीत हुई, हाय! इस तरह कैसे दिन कटेंगे। इन लोगों से तो अलग ही अच्छी थी, पर अलग रहने की भी इच्छा नहीं होती थी, क्योंकि जेल के भीतर, जहाँ अपना कोई रक्षक नहीं, कोई सहायक नहीं, ख़ास तौर से जब अपने कमरों की तालियाँ भी दूसरों के हाथों में रहती हैं, मुझे अकेले रहना मुनासिब न मालूम पड़ा। मैंने हाथ जोड़ कर परमात्मा से प्रार्थना शुरू की—'हे प्रभो! मेरी किसी साथिन को और यहाँ भेज दो।' सम्भवतः मेरी प्रार्थना में बल न था, मुझे घोर तपस्या की ज़रूरत थी, इसलिए मुझे तीन महीने अपनी राजनैतिक क़ैदी बहनों के आने तक ठीक इसी तरह अकेले इन्हीं लोगों की संगति में गुज़ारने पड़े।

जेल में मुझे खाने-पीने की प्रायः कभी तकलीफ़ न हुई। कपड़े मेरे घर से आते थे। पढ़ने के लिए पुस्तकें और लिखने के लिए एक कापी भी मिल गयी थी; सिलाई आदि का सामान भी घर से मँगा लिया था। सप्ताह में एक बार और बाद में दो बार एक हिन्दी अख़बार भी जेल द्वारा मिलने लगा था। पहले एक सप्ताह तक तो खाना बाहर से पक कर आता था, पर उसके बाद मैंने ख़ुद बनाना शुरू कर दिया। अब कोई तकलीफ़ थी तो अकेलेपन की और उन स्त्रियों की बुरी संगति की। मैंने अपना प्रोग्राम बना लिया, और उसी के अनुसार सारा दिन व्यतीत करने लगी, इसी तरह एक सप्ताह जेल में रहते-रहते हो गया।

धीरे-धीरे दिल भी लगने लगा। जेलर को कह देने से अब रात को वॉर्ड भी देर से बन्द होने लगा, इससे सूर्यास्त हो जाने पर बाहर बैठने या घूमने का मौक़ा भी मिल जाता था। गर्मी उन दिनों अधिक थी, दिन भर आँखों से मेहनत करने की वजह से आँखों में रोहे पड़ गये, सर दर्द भी ख़ूब रहने लगा। मैंने सुपरिण्टेण्डेण्ट साहब को अपनी इस बीमारी की सूचना दी, अतः एक दिन प्रातः मुझे दफ़्तर में बुलाया गया। मैं लेडी वॉर्डर के साथ दफ़्तर पहुँची!

मिस्टर रहमान जेल सुपरिण्टेण्डेण्ट दफ़्तर में बैठे थे। उन्होंने मुझसे पूछा—"क्या आप की आँखों में तकलीफ़ है?"

मैं—"जी हाँ।"

मि. रहमान—"क्या तकलीफ़ है?"

मैंने सब तकलीफ़ बतला दी। मि. रहमान ने कहा—"अच्छा, कल या परसों आप की आँखें देखी जायेंगी। शायद आप को ऐनक लेनी होगी।"

मैंने कहा–"मैं किसी विशेषज्ञ; चमबपंसपेजद्ध डॉक्टर से अपनी आँखें दिखाना चाहती हूँ आप कैप्टन टण्डन का प्रबन्ध कर दें, वह आँखों के विशेष डॉक्टर हैं।"

मि. रहमान–"क्यों, ख़ास टण्डन ही क्यों? आप को आँखें दिखाने से मतलब है न कि डॉक्टर से।"

मैं–"मेरा मतलब आँखों के विशेषज्ञ डॉक्टर से है।"

मि. रहमान–"फ़ीस कौन देगा?"

मैं–"मैं जेल में हूँ, मेरा इलाज जेल में नियमपूर्वक होना चाहिए।"

मि. रहमान–"जेल किसी के दाँतों और आँखों का ज़िम्मेदार नहीं।"

मैं–"नहीं, तो नहीं सही। मैं फिर दिखा लूँगी।"

मि. रहमान–"कहाँ से दिखा लोगी?"

मैं–"जब छः महीने बाद जेल से घर जाऊँगी।"

मि. रहमान ने कहा–"अच्छा जाइए।"

मैं चुपचाप अपने वॉर्ड में चली आयी; मुझे चिन्ता थी कि यदि आँखें इसी प्रकार ख़राब होती गयीं तो क्या होगा, पर मैं यह समझती थी कि जेल की यह ड्यूटी है कि मेरी आँखें किसी योग्य डॉक्टर को दिखाई जावें। कुछ दिन बाद सुपरिण्टेण्डेण्ट ने स्वयं ही आँखों के विशेषज्ञ किसी योरोपियन डॉक्टर को ला कर दिखा दीं। मेरे लिए दवा भी तजवीज़ करा दी गयी। अगले दिन कलेक्टर साहब जेल निरीक्षण को आ रहे थे। मैंने प्रायः यही देखा कि जब-जब जेल देखने को कोई अफ़सर आने वाला होता था तो क़ैदियों की माँग पूरी करने का यत्न किया जाता था।

दूसरे दिन प्रातः से ही सारे वार्डों में धूम मच गयी कि साहब आ रहे हैं। क़ैदियों को विशेष सफ़ाई आदि करने की आज्ञा मिली। परेड के लिए लाइनें बनने लगीं। ठीक 9 बजे हमारा वॉर्ड खुला। सुपरिण्टेण्डेण्ट के साथ कलेक्टर साहब ने प्रवेश किया। बिना दूसरी क़ैदिनों को देखे वह मेरी बैरक के पास पहुँचे। मैं खड़ी हो गयी।

कलेक्टर ने पूछा– "क्या आप सकुशल हैं?"

मैं–"जी हाँ।"

कलेक्टर–"कोई तकलीफ़ तो नहीं?"

मैं–"जी नहीं।"

कलेक्टर—"आप इस समय क्या कर रही थीं?"

मैंने अपना तकिया, जिसमें जाली डाल रही थी, दिखा दिया।

कलेक्टर—"अच्छा गुडमॉर्निंग।"

मैं भीतर चली गयी और कलेक्टर दूसरी क़ैदिनों से बिना पूछे ही लौट गये। सुपरिण्टेण्डेण्ट रहमान साहब ने पास से गुज़रती हुई एक क़ैदिन को कुत्ते की तरह दुत्कार ज़रूर दिया। बस, यही उन लोगों की जेल परीक्षा थी।

कलेक्टर के आने के दिन से भी बढ़ कर धूम-धाम का वह दिन था जब जेल में इन्स्पेक्टर जनरल ऑफ़ प्रिज़िन्स (Inspector General of Prisions) अर्थात प्रान्त का सबसे बड़ा जेल का अफ़सर आने वाला था। सारी जेल में सफ़ाई करायी गयी, जगह-जगह लिपाई-पुताई और सफ़ेदी की गयी। दो दिन से जेल के किसी कर्मचारी को दम भरने की फ़ुर्सत न थी। अन्ततः 26 अगस्त को इन्स्पेक्टर जनरल का पदार्पण हुआ। फ़ीमेल वॉर्ड में जब वे आये तो स्वभावतः मुझे उनके आगे पेश किया गया। उन्होंने मामूली प्रश्न किया—"आप अच्छी तरह हैं? किसी चीज़ की ज़रूरत तो नहीं?'

मैं—"अच्छी तरह हूँ। अगर आप चर्खा दिला सकें तो बड़ी कृपा हो, जिसमें मैं कुछ कात कर समय निकाल सकूँ।"

इन्स्पेक्टर जनरल—"चर्खा किसी क़ैदी को नहीं दिया जा सकता!"

मैं—"जहाँ तक मैंने सुना है और जेलों में 'ए' क्लास के क़ैदियों को चर्खा दे दिया जाता है।"

इन्स्पेक्टर जनरल—"अच्छा, हम इसकी ख़बर करेगा और कोई तकलीफ़ तो नहीं?"

मैं—"यहाँ पर मैं अकेली हूँ। पन्द्रह दिन में एक बार मिलना होता है। मुझे चिट्ठी लिखने के बदले एक बार अधिक मिलने की इजाज़त दे दी जाये।"

इन्स्पेक्टर जनरल—"अच्छा, आप को लखनऊ भेज दिया जायेगा, वहाँ आप के साथ की दूसरी औरतें भी हैं।"

इन्स्पेक्टर जनरल इतना कह कर सुपरिण्टेण्डेण्ट के साथ मेरे लखनऊ भेजने के विषय में बातचीत करते हुए चले गये। उनके चले जाने के बाद मैं इस चिन्ता में पड़ गयी कि कहीं सचमुच मुझे लखनऊ भेज दिया तो क्या होगा! लखनऊ जाने की चिन्ता से मैं घबरा उठी। इस में सन्देह नहीं कि एकान्तवास का घोर कष्ट मुझे मेरठ जेल में था, प्रोफ़ेसर जी बार-बार कहते थे कि तुम लखनऊ

चली जाओ तो अच्छा रहे। एकान्तवास का असर मेरे स्वास्थ्य पर भी पड़ रहा था, पर फिर भी मुझे मेरठ से मोह था। मेरे जीवन का नवीन अध्याय मेरठ में प्रारम्भ हुआ था। अपने सुदूरवर्ती कश्मीर के घर को छोड़ कर मैंने मेरठ में अपना घर बनाया था। जेल में होते हुए भी मुझे ऐसा प्रतीत होता था कि मैं घर के नज़दीक हूँ। घर के वायुमण्डल में हूँ, इसलिए मैं मेरठ छोड़ कर लखनऊ जाना नहीं चाहती थी।

अगली बार जब प्रोफ़ेसरजी मिलने आये तो उनसे मुझे यह जान कर बहुत सन्तोष हुआ कि इन्स्पेक्टर जनरल ने मुझे लखनऊ भेजने का विचार छोड़ दिया है। फिर मैंने चर्खे के विषय में पूछा, क्योंकि मैं समझती थी कि मेरे एकान्त जीवन में चर्खा ही एकमात्र सहारा होगा। पर मुझे बताया गया कि इन्स्पेक्टर जनरल ने मुझे चर्खा देने के बदले और जेलों में भी सरक्यूलर भेज दिया कि जिन-जिन सत्याग्रही क़ैदियों को चर्खा दिया गया हो उन सब से छीन लिया जाये! मुझे यह जान कर बहुत दुःख हुआ। इससे तो अच्छा था कि मैं अपने लिए चर्खा न माँगती।

पत्र-व्यवहार के बदले एक अधिक मुलाक़ात करा दी जाये यह बात जेल के नियमानुकूल थी और जेल-मैनुएल में दर्ज थी। मैंने सुना था कि पंजाब की जेलों में ऐसी इजाज़त दे भी दी गयी थी। प्रोफ़ेसरजी ने इस विषय में अख़बारों में भी लिखा और इन्स्पेक्टर जनरल को भी लिखा। परन्तु अन्त में इन्स्पेक्टर जनरल ने गवर्नमेन्ट का ऑर्डर मँगा लिया कि यह क़ायदा 'सी' क्लास वालों के लिए समझा जाये, अर्थात यह 'ए' व 'बी' क्लास वाले सत्याग्रही क़ैदियों पर लागू न हो। पर मुझे अच्छी तरह पता है कि 'सी' क्लास वाले सत्याग्रही क़ैदियों को भी इसका फ़ायदा कभी नहीं दिया गया। अन्त में मैंने यह सोच कर सन्तोष कर लिया कि आख़िरकार हम लोग जेल में कष्ट सहने आये हैं, मेरी तन्हाई भी उस तप का एक भाग है जो हम मातृभूमि के तर्पण के लिए कर रहे हैं।

मेरे दूसरे सत्याग्रही भाइयों को भी एक बात की काफ़ी चिन्ता थी कि मैं जेल के कोने में अकेली पड़ी हुई हूँ। मैंने सुना कि पं. प्यारे लाल शर्मा, क़ाज़ी निज़ामुद्दीन और विशेषकर मौलाना अबुल कलाम आज़ाद ने, जब वे मेरठ जेल आ गये तो इस बात के लिए प्रयत्न किया कि मुझे कभी-कभी अपने सत्याग्रही क़ैदी भाइयों से मिलने की आज्ञा हो जाय। परन्तु जेल के अधिकारियों ने इसे किसी प्रकार स्वीकार नहीं किया। तीन मास तक—जब तक कि दूसरी सत्याग्रही

बहनें जेल में न आयीं–मैंने एकान्त जीवन व्यतीत किया। उन दिनों में मुझे पता चला कि मनुष्य एक सामाजिक प्राणी है, जिस प्रकार उसे रोटी, पानी और हवा की ज़रूरत है, उसी प्रकार अपने साथियों की। उन दिनों में एकान्त जीवन से मुझे कितना ही कष्ट क्यों न हुआ हो, पर आज मैं अनुभव करती हूँ कि एकान्तवास से अपनी विचारधारा में जो उत्तेजना मुझे प्राप्त हुई वह उस कष्ट के बदले पर्याप्त पारितोषिक थी।

मैंने इस परिच्छेद के प्रारम्भ में लिखा है कि मेरी जेल की साथिनों का जीवन किस प्रकार का था। इन लोगों का जीवन कितना घृणास्पद हो जाता है इस की कल्पना करने और देखने में बहुत अन्तर है।

मेरे साथ केवल तीन ही स्त्रियाँ शुरू में थीं जिनमें फ़तहगढ़ में सज़ा काट कर आयी हुई शीघ्र छूट गयी, बाक़ी रहीं दो; उन में एक का शीघ्र ही बच्चा होने वाला था इसलिए उसे काम न करना पड़ता था, दूसरी का काम वॉर्ड में झाड़ू लगाना और मेरे बर्तन आदि धोना था। पर एक समय ऐसा आया जब एक साथ जेल में पन्द्रह स्त्रियाँ हो गयीं। सभी विचाराधीन' अभियुक्त (Under Trial)[1] थीं। ऐसे क़ैदियों के लिए कोई काम देने की आज्ञा नहीं है। अतः उन स्त्रियों में बहुत युद्ध होता था। केवल एक स्त्री झाड़ू लगाने को थी, वह जब झाड़ू लगाती तो तमाम दूसरी क़ैदिनों को गालियाँ देती थी। कभी-कभी तो इसी लड़ाई में साँझ हो जाती थी। जब कभी सुलह रहती–तो सभी स्त्रियाँ मिल-मिला कर प्रातः ही झाड़ू आदि लगा कर ख़ाली हो जातीं। चने बँटने का समय आ जाता। यह भी एक पूरी लड़ाई का सामान था। चने केवल उन्हीं को बँटते हैं जिन्हें सज़ा मिल चुकी हो, बाँटने वाले भी तमाशा देखते थे; किसी एक अण्डरट्रायल को ज़रा-से दे दिये–बस, वहीं सब का मुँह सूज गया; ताने शुरू हुए–"चने बाँटने वालों की आँखों में जो जँच जाये," इत्यादि! उन लोगों में विवेक शक्ति होती ही नहीं, या जेल में पहुँचते ही लोप हो जाती है। संख्या अधिक हो जाने पर प्रायः उन लोगों का निम्न प्रोग्राम रहने लगा!

1. Undertrial- विचाराधीन अभियुक्त अर्थात जिन पर मुक़दमा चल रहा था, पर जिन्हें सज़ा नहीं मिली थी।

प्रातः बैरक खुलने पर उठतीं ओर शौचादि से निवृत हो कर कुछ क़ैदिनें तो मिल-मिला कर झाड़ू लगातीं, शेष ख़ाली एक ओर बैठ कर बातें करतीं। अधिक लड़ाई-फ़साद होने के भय से रोज़ परेड लगाई जाने लगी। जिसका मतलब यह था कि उन सबको एक क़तार में बैठा दिया जाता था और वहीं बैठ कर तरह-तरह की बातें होतीं। चने मिल जाने पर अगर आपस में सब बाँट लेतीं तो शान्ति से बातें होती रहती थीं। कभी-कभी उन्हें अपने घरों की याद आ जाती तो बड़े करुणाजनक शब्दों में अपनी कथा सुनातीं। उस समय मेरा ध्यान भी सुनने में लग जाता था। मुझे एक दिन अपनी ओर आकर्षित देख कर उनमें से एक बोल उठी—''क्या इन्हें जेल आने का दुःख नहीं है?''

दूसरी—''वाह, दुःख कैसे नहीं होगा, जल्दबाज़ी करके आ तो गयीं, पर अब क्या करें।''

पहली—''हाँ, तभी तो जब देखो अलग पड़ी रहती हैं, किसी से बात तक तो करती नहीं।''

इतना कह कर वह स्त्री बड़ी मैत्री-भरे भाव से मेरी ओर देखने लगी। इस पर उनमें एक फिर कहने लगी—''बहन तुमने क्या लेना था, अच्छा ही काम था तो मर्द करते रहते; देखो, दुनिया तो तमाशा देखा करती है, इतने दिन तुम्हें आये हो गये, कोई दूसरी आयी भी?'' मैं इन्हें क्या समझाती!

चने बँटने के बाद रोज़ इसी तरह बातें हुआ करतीं। जब दस बज जाते, कोई स्त्री नहाने जाती, नहीं तो वही गप्पबाज़ी जारी रहती, वही चुग़ली और ईर्ष्या-द्वेष से भरी बातें। कभी हँसतीं और कभी रोतीं, फिर खाना बँट जाता और लेडी वॉर्डर हम लोगों को ताले में बन्द करके खाना खाने के लिए चली जाती। यह समय जेल के रोटी पकाने वालों और जेल वालों को कोसने का हुआ करता था—रोटियाँ कच्ची हैं; दाल गली नहीं; तेल कच्चा डाल दिया है; मिर्च बहुत है। इसी तरह की बीसों बातें कही जातीं। दो बजे तक लेडी वॉर्डर बाहर रहती थी, तब तक सोना और खाना समाप्त हो जाता था। जमादारिन सीधी बैरक में चली आती, वह किसी से सिर दबवाती किसी से पाँव। जो-जो इस सेवा में भाग लेतीं, उनसे जमादारिन का सलूक़ अच्छा रहता था। बीच-बीच नें गाना भी होने लगता था और लेडी वॉर्डर के कहने से नाचना भी। इसी तरह पाँच बज जाते। वॉर्ड खुलता तो सफ़ाई के लिए भंगी भीतर आता। प्रायः उसी के साथ रोटी बाँटने वाले भी आ जाया करते थे। पहले तो रोटी बाँटने के बाद ही वॉर्डर बैरक बन्द

कर जाते थे, पर जब से मैंने एतराज़ किया, वॉर्ड रात को आठ और कभी नौ बजे तक खुला रहने लगा। इस से इन स्त्रियों को भी शाम को खुले आँगन में बैठने का मौक़ा मिलने लगा। खाना ले कर वह सब एक जगह बैठ जातीं और वॉर्ड बन्द होने तक वहीं बैठी बातें करती रहती थीं।

प्रायः लेडी वॉर्डर का पेट भी उन्हीं अभागिनी क़ैदिनों की रोटियों से भर जाता था। जो स्त्री उसे अपनी रोटियों में से एक-दो नहीं दे देती थी, उसको लेडी वॉर्डर की कुदृष्टि का शिकार होना पड़ता था। भोजन के बाद वॉर्ड बन्द हो जाता और रात को पुनः कभी लड़ना, और कभी गाना होता। कभी-कभी वे एक-दूसरे को कहानियाँ भी सुनाती थीं। एक रात एक भूतों की कहानी कहने लगी। सुनाने वालियों में से एक ने कहा—"जमादारिन कहती है कि इस वॉर्ड में जिन पीरजी की क़बर है, वह पीरजी सोमवार और शुक्रवार के दिन नज़र आया करते हैं।"

पहली क़ैदिन—"हाँ, सच तो है। पीरजी बिल्ली की सवारी करते हैं। अगर जुमा या पीर की रात को बारह बजे कोई उठ कर क़बर की ओर देखे तो मालूम हो जाये। उस वक़्त वह क़बर पर नमाज़ पढ़ते हैं। उनकी सवारी इधर-उधर घूमा करती है, तब जो चाहो मुराद माँग लो, पूरी हो जायेगी।"

मैंने कहा—"यह कैसे हो सकता है?"

क़ैदिन—"मैं दिखा दूँगी? जमादारिन से पूछ लेना।" बात दूसरे दिन पर टल गयी। जब दूसरे दिन जमादारिन आयी, तो मैंने पूछा—"क्या यहाँ कोई पीरजी भी आया करते हैं?"

जमादारिन—"हाँ, हमने तो अपनी आँखों देखे हैं। एक क़ैदिन ने जिस पर ख़ून का मुक़दमा था, दिन में ही उन्हें नमाज़ पढ़ते देखा था। वह रोज़ क़बर पर दूध चढ़ाने लगी। पीरजी की उस पर ऐसी मेहरबानी हुई कि वह क़ैदिन साफ़ छूट गयी।"

वह बात तो वहीं समाप्त हो गयी, पर कुछ दिन बाद मैं एक शुक्र की रात को अपनी बैरक में पड़ी सो रही थी। सहसा एक क़ैदिन ने काँपती हुई आवाज़ में मुझे ज़ोर से पुकारा—"बीबी! बीबी!!"

मैंने आधी नींद में पूछा, "क्या है?"

क़ैदिन—"तुम्हारे सिर पर पीरजी की सवारी..." मैं अचानक ऐसा सुनते ही काँप कर उठ बैठी, मैंने देखा मेरे तकिये के पास से एक मोटी-सी बिल्ली निकल गयी। मैं चुपचाप बैठी रही, उस क़ैदिन ने फिर कहा—"बीबी, पीरजी तुम पर ख़ुश

हैं। जो चाहो माँग लो।" मैं तो चुप रही पर उस क़ैदिन ने स्वयं ही माँगना शुरू कर दिया। वह क़ैदिन मुसलमान थी। वह प्रार्थना करने लगी—"ऐ परवरदिगार के दूत! मुझे बख़्श। मेरे दीन भाइयों और बहनों को इन ज़ालिम जेल वालों के फन्दे से छुड़ा।" उस वक़्त उसने नमाज़ पढ़ी और जाने क्या-क्या किया।

मैं वैसी ही बैठी रही, धीरे-धीरे सब मामला समझ में आने लगा। मैंने लेटते-लेटते कहा—

"कुछ भी तो बात नहीं थी, यूँ ही एक बिल्ली लाँघ गयी है।"

ज्यों-ज्यों दिन बीतने लगे, मेरा अनुभव मुझसे बलात कहलवाने लगा कि किसी भी व्यक्ति को चाहे उसने कितना ही भयंकर अपराध किया हो, हिन्दुस्तान की इन जेलों में नहीं भेजना चाहिए। कई बार यह भी ख़याल आता कि ऐसे लोगों के सुधार का क्या उपाय रहेगा। मैं सोचती कि ऐसे शिक्षणालय या कारखाने होने चाहिएँ, जहाँ अच्छे-अच्छे सभ्य लोग आ कर काम सिखायें, पढ़ायें और सदाचार की शिक्षा दें। मैं बैठे-बैठे उत्तम विद्यालयों और कारखानों की कल्पना करने लगती। बड़ा सुन्दर मानसिक चित्र बनाने लगती। कल्पना के चित्र में मुझे नज़र आता कि एक बड़ा विशाल भवन है, जेल ही की तरह उसकी ऊँची-ऊँची दीवारें हैं, पर भीतर से वैसा मैला ओर गन्दा नहीं। स्वच्छ और रमणीय स्थान है। वहाँ अलग-अलग विभाग बने हैं, जहाँ तरह-तरह के काम सिखाने का इन्तज़ाम है, वहाँ क़ैदी साफ़ कपड़े पहन कर रहते हैं। ऐसी ही लम्बी-लम्बी कल्पनाओं के प्रवाह में बह कर मैं अपना समय बिताया करती, पर जब सहसा यह विचार आता कि हम पराधीन हैं, ग़ुलाम हैं, हमारे हाथ में कुछ भी नहीं तो सारा खेल, सारी कल्पना मेरे अन्तःस्तल में लीन हो जाती।

6

संजीवनी सुधा

जेल की प्रत्येक बैरक, यहाँ तक लुहारख़ाना और कुम्हारख़ाना तक, राजनैतिक क़ैदियों से ठसाठस भर चुके थे। राजनैतिक क़ैदियों के जेल के कोने-कोने में फैल जाने से, जेल एक तपोवन-सा बन गया था। प्रातःकाल की शीतल सुगन्धित वायु के साथ ही चारों ओर से राष्ट्रीय गान सुनाई देने लगता था। सभी अपने-अपने वॉर्डों में एक चित्त हो कर मातृ-वन्दना के साथ अपने झण्डे को लिये नित्य नये उत्साह से प्रतिज्ञाएँ किया करते थे। आह! वहाँ वह राग कितना प्यारा लगता था। इस गीत की आवाज़ कान में पड़ते ही जेल का सारा दुःख न जाने कहाँ चला जाता था। जेल के सारे कष्टों में यह राष्ट्रीय गान मेरे लिए संजीवनी सुधा का काम करता था। उसकी तान पर हृदय तन्त्री के तार बज उठते थे और सोती हुई भावनाएँ जाग जाती थीं। गीत उसी तरह चलता जाता था। मैं 'फ़्रीमेल-वॉर्ड' की संकुचित-सी चारदीवारी में बन्द रहती और दीवार के बाहर चारों ओर से राष्ट्र-सैनिकों द्वारा गया जा रहा राष्ट्रीय गीत अस्पष्ट, धीमे परन्तु अत्यन्त मधुर रूप में मेरे कानों में पड़ता था। उस स्वर्गीय गान की एक-एक कड़ी के साथ मेरा दिल नाचने लगता। उस समय ऐसा जान पड़ता जैसे स्वर्ग के देवता मधुर स्वर में मेरी मातृभूमि के राष्ट्रीय झण्डे की स्तुति कर रहे हैं। मैं तन्मय हो कर सुनती, न जाने कौन-कौन मिल कर गा रहे होते थे–

विजयी विश्व तिरंगा प्यारा।
झण्डा ऊँचा रहे हमारा।।
सदा शक्ति बरसाने वाला।

प्रेम सुधा सरसाने वाला।
वीरों को हर्षाने वाला।
मातृभूमि का तन-मन सारा।।
इसकी शान न जाने पाये,
चाहे जान भले ही जाये।
विश्व विजय करके दिखलायें,
तब होवे प्रण पूर्ण हमारा।।
इस झण्डे के नीचे निर्भय,
लें स्वराज वह अविचल निश्चय।
बोलो भारत माता की जय,
स्वन्तत्रता ही ध्येय हमारा।।
प्यारा भारत देश हमारा।। विजयी–

कोई अदृश्य शक्ति मातृभूमि के झण्डे की सम्मान रक्षा के लिए मानो बलात मुझे प्रेरित करती थी। उसी समय गाने वाले अदृश्य देव, गीत की अगली कड़ियाँ गाने लगते थे–

आओ प्यारे वीरो आओ,
देश जाति पर बलि बलि जाओ।
एक साथ सब मिल कर गाओ।।

इस गान में सचमुच विचित्र उत्तेजक शक्ति छिपी है! इसे सुनते ही हृदय उद्वेलित हो जाता था और मैं बार-बार उसी मस्ती में गुनगुनाने लगती थी–

"प्यारा भारत देश हमारा,
झण्डा ऊँचा रहे हमारा।"

बस, ये कड़ियाँ गुनगुनाते ही हृदय पर आनन्द का नशा-सा छा जाता था। मेरा तो जब हृदय अशान्त हो जाता और जब जेल का एकान्त जीवन असह्य हो उठता, तभी यह राग, यह मधुर शक्तिदायिनी सुधा, मेरी उदासी दूर कर मुझे उत्साहित कर देती थी। बैरक में बैठे हुए जब कभी यह राग सुनाई देता था तो

सहसा, बिना इच्छा किये, मैं एक जोश और मस्ती में बैरक से बाहर निकल आती; मुझे कोई प्रबल इच्छा पागल बना देती, जी चाहता कि मैं भी ऊँची आवाज़ में इसी तरह गाऊँ, पर मैं तो अकेली थी। समझ नहीं आता था कि मैं अपनी यह साध कैसे पूरी करूँ।

गाना प्रातः और सायं दोनों समय होता था। अभी एक वॉर्ड से गाने की आवाज़ आ रही होती थी कि दूसरे वॉर्ड वाले भी गाना शुरु कर देते थे। तब सारे जेल में एक ही गीत सुनाई देने लगता था–

''झण्डा ऊँचा रहे हमारा!''

अन्त में अनन्त शान्ति और शक्तिदायक जयघोष होते थे–

'भारत माता की जय हो।'
'तिरंगे झण्डे की जय हो।'

इसके बाद 'वन्दे मातरम' के ऊँचे जयघोष से नौकरशाही का वह कठोर दुर्ग मानो काँप उठता था।

मेरे लिए जेल के सारे कष्टों और मुसीबतों के होते हुए भी यदि कोई आनन्द था तो यही। कोई दिन ख़ाली न जाता था जिस दिन कोई कार्यकर्त्ता या दस पाँच भारतमाता के मतवाले पुत्र इस तपोमय भूमि में स्वतन्त्रता देवी की उपासना करने न आते हों। आने और जाने वालों दोनों ही को स्वागत और विदाई इसी जयघोष के साथ मिला करती थी। दोपहर के ग्यारह बजे से दो बजे तक प्रायः आने वालों के स्वागत की सूचना मिला करती थी। जब तक मेरा कोई साथी नहीं था तब तक मुझे केवल इस राष्ट्रीय गान को सुन कर ही सन्तोष करना पड़ता था; पर उसके बाद जब और बहनें आ गयीं तो फिर प्रातः और सायं हमारे वॉर्ड में भी यही पवित्र पाठ होने लगा और हमारे साथ की साधारण क़ैदी स्त्रियाँ भी इस में सहयोग देने लगीं।

7

ख़ून के आँसू

आह, वह दिन क्या कभी मुझे इस जीवन में भूल सकता है, जब अपनी माँ की गोद में लाड़-प्यार से पले बच्चों को तीस-तीस बेंतों की मार खानी पड़ी थी! मेरे जीवन की स्मृतियों की पुस्तक में वह एक लाल रक्तरंजित पृष्ठ है! उन नवयुवकों के कोमल सुकुमार शरीर जानते भी न थे कि बेंत की चोट क्या होती है। वे अपने किसी पाप से नहीं, बल्कि मातृ-भूमि को प्यार करने के अपराध के कारण जेल में डाले गये थे। उफ़! आज भी मेरा दिल उस याद में काँप उठता है। मुझे ऐसा अनुभव होता है, जैसे अब भी 19 दिन से भूख-हड़ताल किये हुए होने पर भी शान्तिशरण को अभी-अभी बेंतों की सज़ा दी गयी है और उसके कराहने की आवाज़ कानों में गूँज रही है।

29 अगस्त के प्रातः आठ बजे का समय था। सुपरिण्टेण्डेण्ट साहब अपनी मेज़ पर बैठे क़ैदियों का मुलाहिज़ा कर रहे थे, तभी जमादार अशरफ़ अली ने कुछ क़ैदियों के नाम पेश कर दिये। साहब ने पूछा– "क्यों क्या बात है।"

जमादार–"साहब, रात गिनती नहीं होने दी, बहुत तंग करते हैं।"

साहब–"अच्छा, सबको पेश करो।"

अरे, यह क्या? एक बार ही ऊधम-सा मच गया। 'भारत माता की जय' के नाद के साथ ही चीख़ने और चिल्लाने की आवाज़ें आने लगीं मैं चौंक उठी–आज यह नयी बात क्या? मैं दरवाज़े पर खड़ी हुई देखने लगी, पर सिवा शोर के कुछ सुनाई न दिया। अचानक जेल के ख़तरे का घण्टा बजने लगा। क़ैदी शीघ्रता से बैरकों में ठूँसे जाने लगे और शीघ्र ही हुल्लड़ शान्त भी हो गया। जेल में सन्नाटा छा गया। अचानक चीख़ने की आवाज़ें आने लगीं और चीख़ने

से भी ज़्यादा ज़ोर से बेंतों के मारने की सड़सड़ाहट सुनाई देने लगी। किसी ने कहा– राजनैतिक क़ैदियों पर बेंतों की मार पड़ रही है। दिन के बारह बजे थे, ऊपर से धूप आग की तरह बरस रही थी और नीचे तपी हुई पृथ्वी पर सिपाही स्वयंसेवकों के नंगे बदन पर बेंतों की बौछार करने लगे। ख़ून की धराएँ बह निकलीं। मारते-मारते सिपाहियों के बेंत टूटने लगे!

हाय, पीड़ा को भी दया आ गयी, अपनी मोहिनी डाल उसने मार खाने वाले क़ैदियों को एक-एक करके बेसुध कर दिया। प्रकृति ने आँखें बन्द कर लीं। पक्षी यह दृश्य न देख सकने के कारण पास के पेड़ों से उड़ कर दूर चले गये। तब भी बेंतों की और ज़ोर-ज़ोर की गिनती करने की आवाज़ जारी थी। उस दृश्य का वर्णन करना मेरी लेखनी की शक्ति से बाहर है। पर वर्णन करने की अपेक्षा सहज ही में उसकी कल्पना की सकती है। मैंने तो अपने जीवन में वैसा दृश्य कभी देखा ही न था। मैं दौड़ कर फ़ीमेल वॉर्ड के सीकचों के पास जा खड़ी हुई। मेरे हाथों में ताक़त न थी कि उन सीकचों को तोड़ सकूँ। एक साथ ही क्रोध, करुणा और ग्लानि के आवेश में मैं काँप उठीं– मैं असहाय थी, क्या करती? मेरे मुँह से चीख़ें निकल उठीं–हे भगवान, तुम कहाँ हो! उस समय मुझे पता चला कि 'ख़ून के आँसू' किसे कहते हैं। मैं पाषाण के समान स्तब्ध–वहाँ खड़ी हुई थी। इतने में वीर मुख़्तारसिंह की वारी आयी। वॉर्डर ने उसके कपड़े उतार दिये। साहब ने देखा–"ओह, यह तो वही मुख़्तारसिंह है।" लाइन इन्स्पेक्टर ने पहचाना–"हाँ, वही जो पुलिस की नौकरी छोड़ कर कांग्रेस में मिल गया है।" वीर मुख़्तारसिंह को टिकटी से बाँध दिया गया–वीर मुख़्तारसिंह तीस बेंतों के बाद भी होश में था, भारतमाता का पवित्र और शान्तिदायक नाम उस समय भी उसकी जिह्वा पर था। बेंतों की इतनी क्रूर मार के बाद जब लाशों की तरह वे सब वीर फाँसीघर के सामने धूप में पटक दिये गये, तभी दो बजे खाना बँटने के लिए द्वार खुला। पीटे गये अधमरे भाइयों ने अपनी बहन को देखने के लिए प्रार्थना की। द्वार ज़रा-सा खोल दिया गया। मैंने बाहर झाँका–सभी ख़ून में लथपथ थे, कोई होश में और कोई बेहोश नंगी ज़मीन पर वे तेरह वीर पड़े हुए थे। श्री शान्तिशरण के पाँव में तब भी बेड़ी थी, उन्होंने हाथ जोड़ कर लेटे-ही-लेटे कहा– "बहन जी! आज आपके भाई बुरी तरह से पीटे गये हैं।"

मेरे पास कोई शब्द न था, मैं शान्ति भाई से क्या कहती! आह, मैंने तो स्वयं भी इसी पत्थर के कलेजे से उनका आर्त्तनाद सुना था।

मैंने कहा–''मुझे परमात्मा पर विश्वास है। इस घटना का न्याय वही करेगा। बेगुनाहों का ख़ून कभी व्यर्थ नहीं जाता!''

बाद में मुझे अशरफ़ अली ने सारी घटना इस प्रकार सुनाई– ''रात का समय था, हम गिनती करने गये, तो इन लोगों ने गिनती नहीं होने दी। सुबह जब पेशी पर ले जाने लगे तो सारे बैरक के लोग चलने लगे। हमने रोका पर वे माने नहीं। इन्होंने दरवाज़े तोड़ डाले, तब साहब ने ख़तरे का घण्टा बजवा दिया। कलेक्टर साहब ने ख़ुद मौक़ा देख कर उन्हें सज़ा दी है।'' नायब जेलर ने कहा–''फाटक के अस्सी डण्डे तोड़ डाले गये। तन्हाई कोठरियाँ भी तोड़ दीं।''

पर वास्तव में बात क्या थी? रोज़ शाम को जब क़ैदी लोग बैरक से प्रार्थना करने के लिए क़तार बना कर खड़े हो जाते, तभी उनकी गिनती करके बैरकों में भेज दिया जाता था, पर उस दिन (28 अगस्त) को उस समय गिनती नहीं ली गयी, उसके बाद जब रात को सात और आठ के बीच में गिनती करने वॉर्डर पहुँचे और उन्होंने दिन के काम से थके हुए क़ैदियों को बाहर आ कर क़तार में खड़े होने को कहा तो क़ैदियों ने भीतर आ कर गिनती कर लेने की प्रार्थना की। वॉर्डर नहीं माने क़ैदी बाहर निकलने को तैयार नहीं हुए; तब उन्हें हाथ और पाँव से खींच कर बाहर ले जाने का यत्न किया गया। जब इसमें भी सफलता नहीं मिली, तब जैसे-तैसे गिनती कर, कुछ एक के नाम नोट करके वॉर्डर चले गये। क़ैदियों में सबको विश्वास हो गया कि सुबह हथकड़ी, बेड़ी, तनहाई और चक्की आदि का दण्ड मिलेगा। अगले दिन प्रातःकाल जब पेशी के लिए कुछ छाँटे हुए सत्याग्रहियों को पुकारा गया, तो सबने एक साथ बाहर जाने को ज़िद की और सब बाहर निकल कर खड़े हो गये। ऐसी दशा में वॉर्डरों ने उन्हें भीतर बैरकों में बन्द करने का प्रयत्न किया। वे उन्हें धक्के दे-दे कर खींच-खींच कर भीतर ले जाने लगे। साथ ही कई एक क़ैदियों को एक-एक महीना पहले छोड़ देने का लोभ दिया गया, जिससे वह उन क़ैदियों को भीतर डालने में मदद दें, पर परिणाम यह हुआ कि दूसरी बैरकों के क़ैदी भी भाग-भाग कर बाहर आने लगे। इससे चोर, डाकू आदि अन्य क़ैदियों ने यह समझा कि यह समय जेल तोड़ कर भागने का अच्छा है, उन्होंने भी इस गड़बड़ी में भाग लेना शुरू किया। कहा गया था कि सत्याग्रही क़ैदियों ने लोहे के सींकचों के अस्सी डण्डे तोड़ डाले। यह तो बहुत अत्युक्ति थी, पर कुछ अवश्य टूटे थे। परन्तु जिसने मेरठ की जेल 'सी' क्लास की बैरकें देखी हैं, वह कह सकता है कि वह कितनी कच्ची हैं, इतनी

गड़बड़ में इतना शीघ्र निश्चय करना कितना कठिन है कि छड़ें तोड़ने में किसने हिस्सा लिया और किसने नहीं। यह भी याद रखना चाहिए कि राजनैतिक व दूसरे क़ैदी मिला कर रखे जाते थे, और यह कहना कठिन है कि राजनैतिक क़ैदियों ने ही छड़ें तोड़ीं। ख़ासकर शान्तिशरण ने, जो 19 दिन से भूखे तन्हाई की कोठरी में बेड़ी पहने पड़े थे, किस तरह छड़ें तोड़ी होंगी और 16 साल के दुबले-पतले बनर्जी ने छड़ें तोड़ दी हों, मुझे यह असम्भव प्रतीत होता है। फिर इतने लोगों में तेरह क़ैदी और वह भी सारे राजनैतिक किस तरह तीस-तीस बेंतों के लिए छाँट लिये गये। इसके अन्दर क्या भेद है, यह कलेक्टर साहब को ही मालूम होगा।

इस घटना के सम्बन्ध में इतना कह देना अनुचित न होगा कि मेरठ के कलेक्टर मि. पैडले घटनास्थल पर पहुँच गये थे और उन्होंने तीस बेतों की सज़ा का दण्ड दिया था तथा इन्स्पेक्टर जनरल ऑफ़ प्रिज़न्स भी जो जेल का निरीक्षण करने इन दिनों आये हुए थे, जेल के अन्दर विद्यमान थे। परन्तु बेंतों की मार का निरीक्षण भार शायद ज्वॉइण्ट मैजिस्ट्रेट मि. कोगिल पर था जिनकी उपस्थित में 13 सत्याग्रहियों पर तीस-तीस बेंतों की मार पड़ी।

जेल मैनुएल में दिये नियमों के अनुसार जिसके बेंत लगाने हों उसकी शारीरिक अवस्था की डॉक्टरी परीक्षा होनी आवश्यक होती है कि वह बेंत लगाने योग्य है भी या नहीं। जैसा ऊपर कहा जा चुका है कि इस घटना से पहले शान्तिशरण ने 19 दिन का उपवास किया था और वह तन्हाई की कोठरी में बन्द थे और केवल दो दिन पूर्व उपवास तोड़ा था। ऐसी हालत में अन्दाज़ा किया जा सकता है कि शान्तिशरण की क्या दशा हुई होगीं, जब उन्हें तीस बेतों की कठोर सज़ा दी गयी।

इस प्रसंग में यह भी उचित होगा यदि मैं उन सत्याग्रही वीरों के नाम यहाँ अंकित कर दूँ, जिन्हें तीस बेंतों की अमानुषिक सज़ा दी गयी थी–

(१) श्री शान्तिशरण, (२) श्री मनोहरलाल, (३) श्री मुकुन्दलाल, (४) श्री मेघराज, (५) श्री बिहारीलाल (६) श्री श्यामसिंह (७) श्री हरवंश (८) श्री मुख्तारसिंह (९) श्री राजकुमार (१०) श्री भागीरथ, (११) श्री शिताबराय (१२) श्री सूरजभान (१३) श्री बी. एन. बनर्जी

इस घटना के बाद भी जेल में आतंक छाया हुआ था। ऐसा यत्न किया जा रहा था कि जेल की मक्खी भी उड़ कर शहर की ओर न चली जाये, जिससे कि लोगों को इस घटना का पता चल सके।

स्वभावतः इस घटना के बाद मुझे अपने मुलाक़ात के दिन की बड़ी प्रबल प्रतीक्षा हो रही थी। अन्ततः वह दिन आया जिस दिन मेरी मुलाक़ात हुआ करती थी। यह दिन किसी भी क़ैदी के लिए पर्व के दिन से कुछ कम न होता था। मुलाक़ात प्रायः शाम को तीन-चार बजे के बीच में होती थी, पर हम लोग इसकी तैयारी प्रातः से ही करने लग जातीं। दिल में यह विचार आता—आज यह पूछना है; वह चीज़ लाने को कहना है, कौन-कौन मिलने आयेगा। मुझे याद है कि मैं हर बार प्रतीक्षा करती थी कि आज अमुक-अमुक बहन मुझ से मिलने आयेगी। प्रतीक्षा का वक़्त यों ही बहुत लम्बा हुआ करता है, परन्तु उस दिन एक के बाद एक करके पाँच बज गये पर कोई यह कहने नहीं आया—'चलो, मिलने आये हैं।' उफ़! मेरी तबियत भारी होने लगी, क्या वजह है! कहीं बीमार तो नहीं। आह, आज ठीक पन्द्रह दिन के बाद मिलने का समय आया और उसमें भी...मैं कभी बैरक में आती और कभी उड़ कर द्वार की ओर देखने लगती। सहसा द्वार खटखटाया गया। मेरा दिल धड़कने लगा। ज़रूर मेरी बुलाहट है। अपनी घबराहट छिपाने के लिए मैं बैरक में आ कर, व्यर्थ ही एक पुस्तक खोल कर देखने लगी। मैंने देखा द्वार खुला और साथ ही वॉर्डर तथा एक क़ैदी खाने का कच्चा सामान रोज़ की तरह ले कर भीतर आया। मैं प्रतीक्षा करने लगी कि अभी वॉर्डर मुझ से कहेगा—'चलिए,' पर नहीं, वॉर्डर ने केवल यही कहा—"खाने का सामान ले लो।" मैं नहीं कह सकती, कितने यत्न से अपने को सँभाल कर मैंने वॉर्डर से कहा—"मैं सामान अभी नहीं लूँगी।"

वॉर्डर—"क्यों?"

मैंने पूछा—"आज अभी तक मुलाक़ात नहीं हुई, क्या बात है?"

वॉर्डर—"आज आपकी मुलाक़ात नहीं होगी।"

मैं—"क्यों?"

वॉर्डर—"मुझे मालूम नहीं।"

मैं—"पहले मुझे इसकी वजह बतला दी जाये।"

वॉर्डर—"साहब ने मुलाक़ात करनी बन्द करवा दी है, आप किसी से कहिए नहीं।"

मैं—"अच्छा तुम जेलर से कह दो, जब तक मुझे मेरी मुलाक़ात बन्द करवाने की वजह न बतायी जायेगी; तब तक मैं खाना नहीं लूँगी।"

वॉर्डर चला गया। मुझे ऐसा प्रतीत हुआ जैसे धरती घूम रही है। मैं बैठ गयी। इधर जेलर या सुपरिण्टेण्डेट दो-चार दिन से मेरे वॉर्ड में नहीं आये थे, ओर न ही मुझे कोई ऐसी बात ही समझ में आती थी, जिससे मेरी मुलाक़ात रोकी जा सके।

जब तक मैं कुछ सोचूँ, द्वार फिर खुला और एक क्लर्क के साथ वही खाने का सामान फिर से वॉर्ड में आता दिखाई दिया। क्लर्क ने उसी वॉर्डर वाली बात को दुहराते हुए कहा—

"आप खाना ले लें।"

मैं—"पहले मेरे प्रश्न का उत्तर मिलना चाहिए।"

क्लर्क—"जेलर साहब कहते हैं कि आज आपका कोई रिश्तेदार मिलने नहीं आया।"

मुझे पता लग चुका था कि सुपरिण्टेण्डेण्ट की आज्ञा से ऐसा हो रहा है। मैंने कहा—"आप ग़लत कहते हैं। आप लोगों ने मुलाक़ात बन्द की होगी; मुझे ऐसा ख़याल है इसीलिए मैं वजह जानना चाहती हूँ।"

क्लर्क भी वॉर्डर की तरह सामान ले कर लौट गया। मैंने सोचा कि अब मुझे न प्रश्न का उत्तर मिलेगा और न भोजन ही। और अगर कुछ होगा तो यही कि मेरी सुपरिण्टेण्डेण्ट के पास पेशी होगी। पर ऐसा नहीं हुआ। कोई सात बजे के क़रीब नायब जेलर साहब उसी आटे की पोटली को उठवा कर अन्दर आते हुए नज़र आये। उन्होंने आते ही खाना लेने के लिए समझाना शुरू किया; पर मेरे प्रश्न का उत्तर फिर भी नदारद था। हर बार यही उत्तर मिलता कि कोई मिलने नहीं आया। मुझे क्रोध आ गया और मैंने आवेश में कहा—"जेलर साहब, आप लोगों में से किसी को बिना इसका जबाब लिये आने की ज़रूरत नहीं। मैं खाना नहीं लूँगी।" नायब जेलर चला गया।

रात के नौ बज गये; मेरे प्रश्न का उत्तर नदारद था और इसी वजह से मैंने खाने का सामान नहीं लिया। बैरक बन्द होने लगी। मैं भीतर आ कर खाट पर बैठ गयी, इतने में वही क्लर्क आया और कहने लगा—"आपकी मुलाक़ात साहब ने तीन दिन के लिए रोक दी है, केवल आपकी ही नहीं, सारे 'ए' और 'बी' क्लास के राजनैतिक क़ैदियों की और मेरठ कॉनस्पिरेसी-केस वालों की मुलाक़ात भी रोक दी गयी है। मेरा ख़याल है कि अब आपको इससे सन्तोष हो जाना चाहिए। आप अब खाना खा लें। और इतना कह कर बैरक बन्द कर दी गयी। खाने को कह दिया, पर खाने का सामान देना वह भूल ही गया।

चार दिन के बाद फिर हमारी मुलाक़ात का दिन नियत किया गया। नायब जेलर के सामने बैठी मैं अपने सम्बधियों से बातें कर रही थी, बातों में ही प्रोफ़ेसर जी ने मुझ से पूछा—"बर्फ़ आती है या नहीं।"

मैंने कहा—"नहीं, शायद मेरठ कानस्पिरेसी वालों की बन्द हो जाने से मेरी बर्फ़ भी बन्द हो गयी है, क्योंकि शायद ठेकेदार आधा सेर बर्फ़ नहीं लाता होगा।"

साहसा नायब जेलर ने मुझे रोकते हुए कहा—"मिसेज़ शास्त्री, आप यह बात नहीं कर सकतीं, यह जेल की शिकायत है।"

मैं चुप हो गयी, दूसरी बातें होने लगीं मैंने कहा—"मेरी आँखों में रोहे पड़ गये हैं; आजकल पढ़ना-लिखना भी नहीं हो पाता।"

तब फिर प्रोफ़ेसर जी पूछ बैठे—"कैसे हो गये?"

मैंने कहा—"पता नहीं, शायद धूप की गर्मी से। यों तो मैं दिन भर बैरक में रहती हूँ; पर उस दिन जब लड़कों को बेंत लगे, तो बारह बजे से दो बजे तक मैं भी द्वार के पास खड़ी रही थी शायद..."

प्रोफ़ेसर जी ने उत्सुकता से पूछा—"क्या तुमने शान्तिशरण को देखा है? सुना है, उनकी दशा बहुत ख़राब है।"

नायब जेलर ने फिर कहा—"आप यह बात नहीं कर सकते।"

प्रोफ़ेसर जी ने पूछा—"तो कौन-सी बातें कर सकते हैं? हर बात पर आप टोक देते हैं। आप मुझे एक काग़ज़ पर लिख दें, मैं ख़ुद मि. पैडले (कलेक्टर) से पूछ लूँगा कि मुझे अपनी पत्नी से कौन-कौन-सी बातें करने की इजाज़त है।"

नायब जेलर ने कहा—"जो कुछ भी हो आप यहाँ पर पोलीटिकल (राजनैतिक) बातें नहीं कर सकते।"

प्रोफ़ेसरजी —"मैंने जेल मैनुएल अच्छी तरह पढ़ा है। उस में ऐसी कोई पाबन्दी नहीं है कि राजनैतिक बातें नहीं की जा सकतीं।"

नायब जेलर—"मैं जेल मैनुएल नहीं जानता, पर इस प्रकार की बातें आप नहीं कर सकते।"

सचमुच जेल मैनुएल में ऐसी कोई रोक मुलाक़ात के नियमों में नहीं दे रखी थी कि राजनैतिक बातें न की जायें, परन्तु कुछ दिन बाद सरकारी ऑर्डर आ गया और जेल मैनुएल में एक नयी स्लिप जोड़ दी गयी कि क़ैदियों के साथ राजनैतिक बातें मुलाक़ात के समय नहीं की जा सकतीं। इसी झंझट में उस दिन हमारी मुलाक़ात के बीस मिनट भी बहुत जल्दी समाप्त हो गये।

दूसरे दिन सुपरिण्टेण्डेण्ट साहब मेरे वॉर्ड में आये और आते ही बोले–'हैलो मिसेज़ शास्त्री! आप अपने ख़ाविन्द से मिलने के दिन कह देना कि आप से ऐसी बातें न किया करें, नहीं तो आप की मुलाक़ात बन्द करवा दी जायेगी।''

ऐसे भद्दे ढंग से यह बात कही गयी कि मुझे क्रोध आ गया। मैंने कहा– ''आपसे किसने कहा?''

सुपरिण्टेण्डेण्ट–''ज्वालाप्रसाद (नायब जेलर) ने।''

मैंने क्रोध से कहा–''नायब जेलर झूठ बोलता है।''

सुपरिण्टेण्डेण्ट–''मैं हुज्जत नहीं चाहता।''

मैंने भी इसी तरह क्रोध से कहा–''आप हुज्जत नहीं चाहते, मत चाहिए, मुझे भी परवाह नहीं। बड़ी ख़ुशी से मुलाक़ात बन्द करिए, हम तो सहेंगे ही, जो सख़्ती हद से ज़्यादा आप कर सकते हों, करिए। आपको मालूम है, मैं आपके जेल के किसी भी नियम को नहीं तोड़ती और फिर आप एकतरफ़ा सुन कर इस तरह कहने लगे।''

शायद सुपरिटेण्डेण्ट साहब को ख़याल आया हो कि कहीं इसकी आवाज़ जनता में कुछ आन्दोलन पैदा न करे अथवा जेलर ने ही कुछ धीरे से कहा, अतः जाते हुए सुपरिण्टेण्डेण्ट ने मुझसे पुनः पूछा, ''तो क्या बात हुई थी?''

मैंने संक्षेप में बता दिया। तब सुपरिटेण्डेण्ट केवल यह कहते हुए चले गये–''शान्ति का नाम नहीं लेना था।''

इस घटना से पूर्व मुझे कभी नहीं बतलाया गया था कि कौन-कौन-सी बातें मुलाक़ात के समय करनी चाहिएँ या जेल में किन-किन नियमों का पालन होना चाहिए, आदि। केवल देखा-देखी हमें जो नियम मालूम होते रहे, उन्हें ही पालने की चेष्टा मैं करती थी।

8

जेल में क़ैदियों से बर्ताव

कहा जाता है कि हिन्दुस्तान की पुलिस दुनिया भर में सबसे अधिक बिगड़ी हुई है। दुनिया के दूसरे देशों में पुलिस जनता की सहायता और रक्षा के लिए होती है। हिन्दुस्तान में इसके विपरीत पुलिस का काम लोगों को सताना और तंग करना है। अशिक्षित गाँवों में पुलिस का नाम ही डरावना समझा जाता है। पुलिस के समान ही, कदाचित उससे भी बुरी, हालत हिन्दुस्तान की जेलों की है। पहले तो जेल के क़ायदे-क़ानून ही सख़्त हैं, तिस पर भी उन्हें बेरहमी से काम में लाया जाता है। पर साथ ही मेरा यह अनुभव है कि जेल की सख़्त आज्ञाओं और नियमों के होते हुए भी जहाँ अच्छा या बुरा व्यवहार होना किसी भी अच्छे या बुरे स्वभाव वाले अधिकारी पर निर्भर है, वहाँ जैसा चाहें वैसा व्यवहार करवाने का भार क़ैदियों पर सारा नहीं तो कुछ-न-कुछ ज़रूर है। यों तो जान-बूझ कर अच्छे स्वभाव वाले आदमी जेल के अधिकारी ही नहीं बनाये जाते और यदि बनते भी हैं तो दूसरे लोगों से मिल कर वह भी बिगड़ जाते हैं। कठिनता से कोई ऐसा सुपरिण्टेण्डेण्ट या जेलर होगा, जो किसी भी झगड़े की जाँच मेहनत से ठीक-ठीक करे। क़ैदियों की शिकायत जैसी वॉर्डरों ने कर दी; सुपरिण्टेण्डैण्ट या जेलर ने वैसा ही सुन लिया। अगर सुपरिण्टेण्डेण्ट दूसरे क़ैदियों से गवाही भी माँगे, तो वही गवाही देंगे जो वॉर्डर उन्हें पहले से याद करा चुके हों। अगर क़ैदी ऐसा न करे तो वॉर्डर बैरक में जा कर उनकी बुरी गति करते हैं। बात-बात में तनहाई, बेड़ी आदि का उपहार दिलवाने लगते हैं। जिसके डर के मारे हर एक को वॉर्डरों को प्रसन्न रखने की चेष्टा करनी पड़ती है। वॉर्डर जितनी तनख्वाह पाते हैं उससे कई गुनी अधिक क़ैदियों से प्राप्त करते हैं। किसी मुलाक़ात के समय जिसने

वॉर्डर को चुपके से कुछ रुपये आदि दिला दिये, वह तो ठीक, नहीं तो मार-पीट, तनहाई आदि सज़ा से बदला लिया जाता है।

मुझे याद है कि मेरे छूटने से कुछ दिन पूर्व एक मुसलमान लेडी वॉर्डर रखी गयी थी। वह एक दिन हमारे वॉर्ड की एक 'सी' क्लास की स्त्री की मुलाक़ात कराने को ले गयी। उस स्त्री की एक छोटी लड़की और उसका एक चार वर्ष का लड़का अपनी माँ से मिलने आया था। माँ को देखते ही बच्चे चिल्ला-चिल्ला कर रोने लगे; इधर माँ भी रो रही थी। देखने वालों का दिल फटा जा रहा था, पर वह हृदयहीन लेडी वॉर्डर माँ और बच्चों के बीच खड़ी हो गयी। उसने कहा, ''मुझे कुछ दिलवाओ।'' लड़की ने कहा—''मेरे पास केवल चार आने हैं, यहाँ से अपने गाँव तक जाना होगा, अगर तुम्हें दे दूँ तो इक्केवाले को क्या दूँगी।'' परन्तु लेडी वॉर्डर ने एक ही रट लगा रखी थी, ''नहीं, तुम्हें देने ही होंगे। चली थी मिलायी करने और पल्ले दाम तक नहीं; ऐसे थोड़े ही मिलायी होती है।'' क़ैदी स्त्री ने हाथ जोड़ कर कहा—''वक़्त जा रहा है, दो बात कर लेने दो।'' पर वॉर्डर को तो दाम चाहिए थे। लड़की ने चार पैसे निकाल कर सामने रख दिये, पर वॉर्डर न हटी—''क्या चार पैसे के लिए मैं तुम्हें यहाँ तक लायी हूँ।'' क़ैदिन माँ ने रोते हुए अपनी लड़की से कहा—''दे डाल बेटी, रास्ते में भीख माँगती हुई चली जाना, नहीं तो आज के बाद तीन महीने तक मिलायी नहीं हो सकेगी।'' लड़की ने आँचल से दाम खोल कर लेडी वॉर्डर की ओर बढ़ा दिये। वॉर्डन ने धीरे से जूता उतार कर कहा कि इसमें डाल दो, होशियारी से, कोई देख न ले।'' पैसे डलवा कर माँ और भी ज़्यादा रोने लगी—''हाय, आज मेरे बच्चों को भूखे-प्यासे तो लौटना होगा ही, पर मेरे जीते भीख भी माँगनी पड़ेगी।'' कितना करुण दृश्य था, साधारण मनुष्य तो माँ और बच्चों के इस मिलन को देख कर पिघल जाय, पर जेल कर्मचारियों के जिस्म में विधाता ने वह चीज़ डाली ही नहीं जिसे दिल कहते हैं।

साधारणतया जेल के अधिकारियों का स्वभाव क्रूर और कठोर होता है। जब कोई क़ैदी अपनी अधिकार-रक्षा के लिए या अपने ऊपर होते हुए अन्यायपूर्ण अत्याचार के विरुद्ध कुछ कहने का यत्न करता है, तब तो इस क्रूरता का नंगा रूप प्रकट हो जाता है।

सबसे बड़ी कठिनता का सामना बेचारे अशिक्षित क़ैदियों को इसलिए करना पड़ता है कि उन्हें जेल के नियम का पता नहीं होते। जेल में रहने वाले क़ैदी

और विचाराधीन अभियुक्त, दोनों के ही लिए जेल के नियम होते हैं। परेड कैसे करना चाहिए, अपनी आवश्यकताओं को अफ़सर तक कैसे पहुँचाना चाहिए, किस ढंग में रहना बैठना और चलना-फिरना चाहिए, आदि इन नियमों को आने वाले नये क़ैदी को यह बता देना कितना आवश्यक है। अफ़सर लोग कभी यह पूछने व जानने की चेष्टा नहीं करते है कि अपराधी के अपराध करने का कारण क्या है। मैंने देखा बेक़ायदा रहने और काम करने के कारण रोज़ ही बीस-बीस और पच्चीस-पच्चीस क़ैदियों को सुपरिण्टेण्डेण्ट हथकड़ी, बेड़ी, तनहाई का दण्ड देते थे। सज़ा देते समय बेचारे क़ैदी से कुछ पूछना आवश्यक न समझा जाता था। उन दिनों प्रायः यह शिकायत सबसे ज़्यादा रहती थी, क़ैदी नियम तोड़ते हैं; पर कभी किसी ने यह भी सोचा कि उन्हें नियम बताये किसने थे। उदाहरण ाार्थ–क़ैदी को चाहिए कि अपनी ज़रूरत परेड के दिन सुपरिण्टेण्डेण्ट के सामने कहे और वह भी पहले हाथ उठा दे। जब कोई उससे पूछे क्या चाहते हो, तब वह अपनी ज़रूरत को कहे। ऐसा नियम शिक्षित क़ैदी तो एक-दूसरे को देख कर भी समझ जाते हैं, पर 'सी' क्लास में अधिकतर गाँव के अशिक्षित होते हैं, जब तक उन्हें बताया या समझाया न जाये, वे कैसे जानें? वे लोग साहब के आने पर बिना हाथ उठाये या बिना पूछे, बोलने लगते थे, जिस पर साहब कहते थे–बेतरीक़े क्यों बोला, नाम नोट करो, हमारे सामने पेश करना। बेचारे क़ैदी मन-ही-मन जला करते, पर बेचारे क्या कर सकते थे।

जेल के सुपरिण्टेण्डेण्ट कर्नल रहमान को किसी बात की चिन्ता थी तो अपना रौब जमाने की। बड़ी शान से वह क़ैदियों के वॉर्ड में आते थे। साहब के वॉर्ड आने की सूचना उनका कुत्ता दिया करता था, जिसे वह सदा साथ रखते थे, हालाँकि जेल में कुत्ता लाना जेल के नियम के विरुद्ध है। उसके बाद जेलर, डॉक्टर और एक सी. आई. डी. के आदमी के साथ सुपरिण्टेण्डेण्ट साहब वॉर्ड में प्रवेश करते थे; उनके ठीक पीछे चँवर हाथ में लिये और सुपरिटेण्डण्ट साहब की पीठ पर बैठने वाली मक्खियों को उड़ाते हुए एक नम्बरदार होता था, जिसके पीछे पुलिस के दो सिपाही और वॉर्डर होता था। हमारे वॉर्ड में आते हुए उन्हें शायद अपनी जान का इतना भय नहीं था, इसलिए दोनों सिपाही वॉर्ड के द्वार पर ही रह जाते थे। सुपरिण्टेण्डेण्ट साहब हिन्दुस्तानी होते हुए भी हम लोगों से अंग्रेज़ी में सिर्फ़ इसलिए बोलते थे कि जिसमें हमें ख़याल हो जाये कि आप हिन्दुस्तानी बोली नहीं जानते। मैंने कई बार कहा–मेरे साथ हिन्दुस्तानी में बात किया करें,

पर उन्हें बड़ी कठिनता मालूम पड़ती थी। बेचारे जेलर से अंग्रेज़ी शब्दों के अर्थ पूछा करते थे। यदि कोई अंग्रेज़ सुपरिण्टेण्डेण्ट होता, तो दूसरी बात थी। पर यहाँ तो एक हिन्दुस्तानी महाशय थे जिन्हें अपनी बोली बोलने में मुश्किल होती थी। शायद कोई अंग्रेज़ टूटी-फूटी हिन्दुस्तानी बोल लेता, पर हमारे देशी साहब को बिना जेलर की सहायता के हिन्दुस्तानी बोलने में शर्म आती थी। यह है, हमारे भाग्य की विडम्बना, यह है हमारी ग़ुलामी का, हमारी मानसिक दासता का लज्जापूर्ण चित्र! जब मेरे साथ ही साहब को हिन्दुस्तानी बोलने में इतना संकोच होता था तो बेचारे 'सी' क्लास के अंग्रेज़ी का अक्षर न जानने वालों के साथ क्या बात करते होंगे? हाँ, बात-बात पर डाँट देना, बुरी तरह बात करना, उनका विशेष स्वभाव प्रतीत होता था। उन्होंने कभी मेरा ही लिहाज़ न किया, तब वह किसी पुरुष का क्या लिहाज़ करते।

जब तक जेल के सुपरिण्टेण्डेण्ट कर्नल अब्दुल रहमान रहे, मुझे एक ख़ास शिकायत उनके समय में रही; वह न स्वयं कभी नियम बनाते और न दूसरों का ही ख़याल करते थे। उन्होंने अपने समय में महिला वॉर्ड में निरीक्षण के लिए आने का दिन या समय कभी निश्चित नहीं किया, वह करते क्यों? वह तो अपने को जेल का परमेश्वर समझते थे। कभी-कभी तो जब मैं नहा रही होती थी तभी दरवाज़ा खटकने लगता था; वॉर्डर चिल्लाती, "साहब बहादुर आते हैं!" इधर मैं चिल्लाती थी, "जमादारिन, ठहर जाओ।" द्वार खुल जाता था और मुझे जल्दी से बिना नहाये ही कपड़े पहन कर सामने आना पड़ता था। कई बार चाहा कि रहमान साहब कम-से-कम आने से आध घण्टे पहले सूचना ही भिजवा दिया करें, पर ऐसा कभी न हो सका। मुझे निःसंकोच कहना पड़ेगा कि उनके बाद जब एक यूरोपीय व्यक्ति मेजर क्लाइड सुपरिण्टेण्डेण्ट बन कर आये, तो हमारी यह तकलीफ़ सदा के लिए दूर हो गयी। परन्तु रहमान साहब जब कभी भीतर आये, उन्होंने इस बात की परवाह नहीं की कि मैं एक सभ्य स्त्री के सामने बात कर रहा हूँ जो साधारण क़ैदी नहीं प्रत्युत राजनैतिक क़ैदी है।

मुझे यह कहते हुए कुछ लज्जा आती है कि जहाँ एक ओर एक हिन्दुस्तानी सुपरिण्टेण्डेण्ट का यह बरताव था, वहाँ दूसरी ओर योरोपियन सुपरिण्टेण्डेण्ट ने एक भद्र महिला के प्रति जो मान-मर्यादा दिखानी चाहिए उसका सदैव ध्यान

रखा। मेरे रहते हुए जेल में दो योरोपियन सुपरिण्टेण्डेण्ट आये—एक मेजर यूल (एक फ़ौजी अंग्रेज़) जो कर्नल रहमान के सात दिन तक छुट्टी जाने पर उनके स्थान में आये और दूसरे मेजर क्लाइड जो स्थायी रूप से कर्नल़ रहमान की बदली होने पर उनकी जगह आये। दोनों ही का व्यवहार मेरे प्रति कितना शिष्टता और सभ्यता से पूर्ण था। उसमें और एक हिन्दुस्तानी सुपरिण्टेण्डेष्ट के व्यवहार में कितना अन्तर था। जब कभी मैं इस पर विचार करती तो मेरा मन क्षुब्ध हो उठता। मैं सोचती कि हमारे भाई इसी प्रकार के शासक हुआ करेंगे। बहुधा मैंने सुना था कि हिन्दुस्तानी अफ़सर और अंग्रेज़ अफ़सरों के चरित्र में बड़ा फ़र्क़ होता है, पर यहाँ तो बात स्वयं मेरे ऊपर आ पड़ी और मैंने देखा कि हमारे भाइयों का कितना पतन हो चुका है, इस पर विचार करते-करते मुझे ख़याल आया कि यह सब ग़ुलामी की नियामतें हैं। महात्मा गाँधी ने ठीक ही कहा है कि सब से बड़ा अनर्थ जो विदेशी राज्य से हुआ है, वह आर्थिक पतन नहीं, बल्कि हमारा मानसिक और नैतिक पतन है। एक योरोपियन अफ़सर चाहे दुश्मनी का भाव ही रखे, पर वह आज़ादी की क़ीमत जानता है। चाहे वह ऊपर से अपने भाव को कितना ही छिपा ले, पर अपने हृदय की तह में वह आज़ादी के सिपाहियों की इज़्ज़त किये बिना नहीं रह सकता, पर एक हिन्दुस्तानी सरकारी नौकर की हालत दूसरी है। उसे पता नही कि आज़ादी क्या वस्तु है। उसका दित और दिमाग़ जिस धातु से बना है। उसका नाम है—ग़ुलामी!

9

कीचड़ में कमल

साधारण नियमों में अपवाद होना ईश्वर की सृष्टि का एक निश्चित विधान है, अपवादों के बिना शायद यह जगत बहुत कठोर और असत्य बन जाता। काली अँधेरी रात में एक प्रकाश की रेखा, बिजली चमक उठती है; समुद्र की गँदली अँधेरी सतह में चमकदार मोती बिखरे हुए हैं; कीचड़ में कमल खिलता है, और वीरान रेगिस्तान में हरियाली अंकुरित होती है। जेल जैसे नारकीय स्थानों में भी भगवान की विभूति की झलक कभी-न-कभी मिल ही जाती है। मैंने कहा है कि जेल के लोग कितने क्रूर और निर्दय होते हैं, परन्तु वहाँ भी ऐसी पवित्रात्माएँ पहुँच ही जाती थीं जिनके चेहरे पर दया और सहानुभूति अंकित होती है। यों तो जेल में समय-समय पर एक-दो ऐसे कर्मचारी आते ही रहे जिनमें मनुष्यता थी और जिनका व्यवहार सदैव शिष्ट होता था, परन्तु जिस व्यक्ति को देख कर मुझे असीम आश्चर्य और हर्ष हुआ, वह था एक बूढ़ा वॉर्डर। मेरी कितनी इच्छा होती है कि मैं उसका नाम यहाँ अंकित कर दूँ, परन्तु वैसा करना शायद उस ग़रीब के लिए हानिकारक होगा।

मैं एक दिन बड़ी घबराहट और निराशा से विकल हो रही थी। वह जब फ़ीमेल वॉर्ड की ओर आया तो बातचीत में मैंने कहा कि मुझे और तो कोई कष्ट नहीं, पर यह चिन्ता अवश्य रहती है कि मैं यहाँ अकेली राजनैतिक क़ैदिन हूँ। इतना सुनते ही उसने कहा—"बहन जी, इससे आपको ज़रा-सी भी चिन्ता न करनी चाहिए। यदि ज़रूरत पड़े तो मैं नौकरी को भी तिलांजलि दे डालूँगा।"

वह उन व्यक्तियों में से न था, जो लम्बी-चौड़ी बातें कह डालते हैं। उसने जो कुछ कहा, उसका एक-एक शब्द उसके हृदय से निकला था। उसक चेहरे से

वह भाव टपकता था जो धर्मात्मा और सत्यवादियों के चेहरों पर सदा झलकता रहता है। कहना न होगा उसके आने के बाद मुझे कभी किसी प्रकार की चिन्ता और घबराहट न रही। मैं आश्चर्य में पड़ी हुई सोचने लगी कि इस नरक में भी आतताइयों से रक्षा करने के लिए रक्षक देवदूत विद्यमान हैं।

एक दिन तो उस वॉर्डर ने मुझे सचमुच आश्चर्य में डाल दिया। जेल में 'ए' और 'बी' श्रेणी के क़ैदियों के जो फलादि आते हैं, वे बहुधा अधिक होने पर जेल के कर्मचारी सिपाही वॉर्डर आदि को मिल जाते हैं। मेरे सामान पर तो लेडी वॉर्डर की ख़ास नज़र रहती थी और मैं भी प्रायः उसे दे दिया करती थी।

एक दिन मेरे घर से कुछ फल आदि आये थे। वह बूढ़ा वॉर्डर उन दिनों बीमार था। डॉक्टर ने उसे केवल दूध और फल खाने को कह रखा था। मैं जानती थी कि बाल-बच्चेदार वॉर्डर बीस रुपये में अपने लिए दूध-फल नहीं जुटा सकता। मैंने सोचा अगर कुछ दिनों के लिए दूध और फल वॉर्डर को दे दिया करूँ तो बेचारे को फ़ायदा हो। एक दिन कुछ फल वॉर्डर को देते हुए मैंने कहा—"तुम रोज़ मेरा दूध ले लिया करो।" मैं कितने आनन्द और आश्चर्य से उसका मुख ताकती हुई रह गयी जब उसने निम्न शब्दों के साथ मेरी सब चीज़ें वापस कर दीं—"बहन जी! मैंने कभी अपनी बड़ी बहन तक के घर का नहीं खाया, आप तो मुझसे बहुत छोटी हैं। हिन्दू के लिए तो छोटी बहन के घर का खाना पाप लिखा है।"

उस दिन से मेरी श्रद्धा उस वॉर्डर पर हो गयी। मुझे उस समय कितना आनन्द हुआ होगा, वह कोई कोई मेरी अवस्था में पड़ा हुआ व्यक्ति ही अनुभव कर सकता है!

10

जेल में मेरी बीमारी

सारे दिन जेल की चहारदीवारी और रात को कमरे में बन्द रहने का असर मेरे स्वास्थ्य पर पड़े बिना नहीं रह सकता था। यदि कोई स्त्री जो आजकल की कठोर पर्दा प्रथा की शिकार हो कर घर में लगातार बन्द रहती है, इस प्रकार एक जगह बन्द कर दी जाती तो शायद उसके लिए यह कोई बड़ा अन्तर न होता, पर मैंने अपना सारा जीवन खुली हवा में बिताया था, कश्मीर के स्वच्छ वायु-मण्डल में घूमते हुए मैं इतनी बड़ी हुई थी। एक साथ ही तंग जगह में बन्द होने से जो मानसिक कष्ट होता उसे तो मैं ज्यों-त्यों करके उच्च भावनाओं से दबाने की चेष्टा करती पर शरीर पर तो उसका असर पड़ना ही था। फल यह हुआ कि जेल में दो मास तक रहने के बाद मुझे हल्का-सा ज्वर होना शुरू हो गया। प्रतिदिन शाम को 99 और कभी 100 डिग्री तक बुख़ार हो जाता। जब पन्द्रह-बीस दिन तक यही हालत रही तो मुझे और मुझसे बढ़ कर मेरे घर के लोगों को इसकी चिन्ता होने लगी।

मुझे किसी लेडी डॉक्टर को दिखाने का प्रश्न उपस्थित हुआ। मैंने कहा कि मैं अब तक लेडी डॉक्टर मिसेज़ टण्डन से अपना इलाज कराती रही हूँ, उन्हें ही बुला कर मुझे दिखा दिया जाये। उस समय कर्नल रहमान की जगह मेजर यूल एक सप्ताह के लिए काम करने आये हुए थे। उन्होंने मेरी प्रार्थना पर मिसेज़ टण्डन को बुलाना स्वीकार कर लिया; पर जब जेलर को यह पता लगा तो जेलर ने मेजर यूल से कहा कि मिसेज़ टण्डन को बुलाना कर्नल रहमान को कभी पसन्द न आयेगा। पता यह चला कि कर्नल रहमान और कैप्टन टण्डन में कुछ अनबन हो चुकी थी जिसके कारण जेल में मिसेज़ टण्डन को भी नहीं बुलाया जा सकता

था। अन्त में मेजर यूल अपने साथ एक लेडी डॉक्टर को लाये जिसका नाम मिस जॉन था। उन्होंने अच्छी तरह मेरी परीक्षा करके मेरे लिए दवाई तजवीज़ कर दी। दवाई बन कर भी आ गयी और जेल की व्यवस्था के अनुसार मैं उसे पीने लगी, पर वहाँ कोई यह देखने वाला नहीं था कि वह दवाई मुझ पर क्या असर कर रही है—बुरा या भला? वह तो एक बार बन कर आयी, फिर जेल के क़ायदे के अनुसार बोतल समाप्त करनी मेरे लिए आवश्यक थी। फल यह हुआ कि मेरी दुर्दशा कुछ सुधरी नहीं, बल्कि बिगड़ती ही गयी।

यह बात अक्टूबर मास की है। उन्हीं दिनों में कर्नल रहमान के बदले जेल में योरोपियन महाशय, मेजर क्लाइड सुपरिण्टेण्डेण्ट बन कर आये। जैसा कि मैं पूर्व भी लिख चुकी हूँ, उन्होंने मेरे साथ बहुत सहानुभूति का व्यवहार किया, और शास्त्री जी के आग्रह करने पर यह भी स्वीकार कर लिया कि मेरी शारीरिक परीक्षा मेरठ के सुप्रसिद्ध चिकित्सक डॉ. भूपाल सिंह जी के द्वारा करायी जावे। तदनुसार डॉ. भूपाल सिंह जी ने जेल में आ कर मुझे देखा, उनके देखने से सबसे बड़ा लाभ यह हुआ कि कम-से-कम मुझे और मेरे सब सम्बन्धियों को सन्तोष हो गया।

इन्हीं दिनों में यह व्यवस्था कर दी गयी कि मैं प्रति सप्ताह एक बार मेरठ शहर के ज़नाने अस्पताल में चिकित्सा के लिए भेजी जाया करूँ। मुझे याद है कि जिस दिन मैं पहली बार जेल की चहारदीवारी से निकल कर मेरठ शहर में होती हुई ज़नाने अस्पताल में लायी गयी तो उस समय मेरे हृदय में एक साथ ही न जाने कितने अपूर्व भाव उठ रहे थे। मैं एक लॉरी में तेज़ी के साथ शहर से निकाल कर अस्पताल पहुँचा दी गयी। लॉरी में चार सिपाही तैनात रहते थे—शायद मैं भाग न जाऊँ! फलतः जेल का सारा वायु-मण्डल मेरे चारों ओर था, परन्तु फिर भी एक बार खुली हवा में आने से केवल मेरठ की सड़कों पर दृष्टि डालने की क्षमता प्राप्त होने से मेरे हृदय को जो अनिर्वचनीय आह्लाद हुआ, उसे मैं किन शब्दों में लिख सकती हूँ। मैं सोचने लगी कि पराधीनता भी कितनी मधुर है। फिर सचमुच वह दिन भारत के इतिहास में कितना उज्ज्वल होगा जिस दिन सदियों की ग़ुलामी के बाद भारत के वायु-मण्डल में स्वाधीनता का प्रथम प्रभात चमकेगा।

मैं अपने विषय से दूर चली गयी; सचमुच उस समय तो एक प्रकार से मैंने अपनी बीमारी को धन्यवाद दिया। लॉरी में जल्दी से निकलते हुए कई भाइयों

की दृष्टि मुझ पर पड़ती थी, पर वे लोग संभ्रम में पड़ जाते। कई भाई मुझे नमस्कार करते, परन्तु पूर्व इसके कि मैं उसका उत्तर दूँ लॉरी आगे निकल जाती। लगभग आध घण्टे अस्पताल में रह कर फिर मैं जेल में वापस चली जाती। साधारणतया मेरे अस्पताल जाने का दिन बुधवार था, परन्तु पीछे शायद इस दृष्टि से कि निश्चित दिन होने से मेरे सम्बन्धी मुझे अस्पताल मिलने न पहुँच सकें, दिन अनिश्चित रहने लगा और किसी समय अकस्मात बिना पूर्व सूचना के मुझे अस्पताल जाने के लिए बुलावा आ जाता था। जो कुछ भी हो, प्रति सप्ताह एक बार अस्पताल जाने से मुझे कुछ-न-कुछ लाभ अवश्य प्रतीत हुआ, पर यह नहीं कह सकती कि वह लाभ ज़नाना अस्पताल की दवाई से हुआ या चार मास के बन्दी को खुली हवा के दो-चार झोंकों के लगने से।

इस प्रसंग में यह अनुचित न होगा यदि मैं इस परिच्छेद में दो-चार शब्द जेल की चिकित्सा और जेल के अस्पताल के विषय में लिखूँ। यद्यपि मुझे आँखों से जेल के अस्पताल के कमरे देखने का कभी मौक़ा नहीं मिला, पर जेल के डॉक्टर और कम्पाउण्डर हमारे वॉर्ड में औषधि देने और हाल पूछने प्रायः रोज़ आते थे। जेल-नियम के अनुसार उन लोगों को रोज़ एक बार प्रत्येक वॉर्ड में जाना ज़रूर होता था। केवल बीस या पच्चीस दिन छोड़ कर (जिन दिनों जेल में मलेरिया फैला हुआ था) क़ैदियों की संख्या चाहे 1000 हो या 400, पर वही एक डॉक्टर और वही एक कम्पाउण्डर काम करते थे। मलेरिया के दिनों में कभी-कभी एक-आध कम्पाउण्डर और भी आये, पर 24 घण्टे से ज़्यादा कोई ठहर न सका, जिसका कारण सुनने में यही आता था कि उनसे कहा गया कि पहले कुछ दिन अवैतनिक काम करो तो फिर देखा जायेगा, पर वस्तुतः अवैतनिक रूप में काम करने को कोई तैयार न होता था।

जेल की दवाइयाँ भी ख़ास पेटेण्ट थी, एक बोतल से भरा हुआ पानी न जाने कितनी बीमारियों का इलाज था। वहाँ दवाइयों के नम्बर मुक़र्रर थे। अब ठीक तो याद नहीं आ रहा, पर शायद उस लाल पानी का नम्बर 40 था। मैंने देखा, हमारे वॉर्ड में अगर किसी को सर दर्द है, पेट दर्द या और कोई साधारण दर्द आदि है तो वही लाल रंग का पानी हर-एक को दिया जा रहा है; एक नाप के गिलास में वहाँ पानी भर के लाया जाता था। किसी ने कहा मुझे ज़ुकाम है तो वही एक डोज़ पिला दी और किसी ने कहा पेट दर्द करता है तो उसी में से दूसरा डोज़ पेट-दर्द के लिए भी औषधि हो गया, और वही सर दर्द के काम भी आ जाता था।

चिकित्सा की यह हालत होने के कारण जेल में कभी-कभी बड़ा अनर्थ भी हो जाता था। एक बार मैंने सुना कि एक बुड्ढा क़ैदी बीमार पड़ गया। अस्पताल के कमरे में ही रात को उसकी हालत बहुत ख़राब हो गयी। हाथ-पाँव ठण्डे होते देख एक क़ैदी ने वॉर्डर से कहा "कम्पाउण्डर साहब या डॉक्टर साहब को ख़बर कर दो।" ख़बर हो गयी; पर वहाँ से जवाब मिला, "अगर ऐसी हालत है, तो मर गया होगा, देख कर एक अलग खाट पर डाल दो, मैं ही जा कर क्या कर लूँगा।" बेचारे बूढ़े क़ैदी को निमोनिया का बुख़ार एकदम दूर हो जाने से शिथिलता के मारे बेहोशी-सी हो गयी थी। बेचारा अलग खाट पर डाल दिया गया, जहाँ वह प्रातः आठ बजे तक पड़ा रहा पर किसी ने नहीं देखा कि वास्तव में मरा है या नहीं। ठीक 9 बजे सुपरिण्टेण्डेण्ट अस्पताल में दाख़िल हुए। उन्हें सूचना दी गयी कि एक क़ैदी रात को मर गया, परन्तु साहब ने जब कपड़ा हटाया तो क़ैदी की साँस चल रही थी, उसे उठा कर कमरे में लाया गया। रात की सर्दी से बेचारा बुड्ढा क़ैदी काँप रहा था और उसी कँपकँपी में उसके प्राण दोपहर के दो बजे शरीर से अलग हो गये।

जिस झाड़न से औषधियाँ ढँक कर लायी जाती थीं, वह प्रायः मैला होता था; वह जेल में ही साधारणतया धो दिया जाता था; धोबी का घर तो उसने कभी देखा ही न था। ऐसी अवस्था में यदि क़ैदी जीते रहे तो अपने भाग्य से। इसलिए यदि जेल में जा कर जिसे बदक़िस्मती से एक-आध बार भी ज्वर आया तो बस वह फिर सँभला तो अपने घर जा कर।

11

प्रतिष्ठित अभ्यागत महिलाएँ

साधारणतया जब 15वें दिन मेरी मुलाक़ात होती थी, उस समय कभी मेरठ की और कभी बाहर की मेरी सम्बन्धिनी स्त्रियाँ मुझसे मिलने आया करती थीं, परन्तु दो बार ऐसा अवसर आया जब कि कुछ प्रतिष्ठित महिलाएँ जेल सुपरिण्टेण्डेण्ट के द्वारा विशेष प्रबन्ध करके मुझे से जेल की बैरक में मिलने आयीं।

एक दिन कर्नल अब्दुल रहमान मेरी बैरक में आये और मुझ से कहने लगे कि कुछ औरतें आप को जेल में देखना चाहती हैं। किसी अंग्रेज़ महिला से मिलने में आप कोई आपत्ति तो न होगी या केवल आप हिन्दुस्तानी स्त्रियों से ही मिलती हैं। मुझे उनके प्रश्न पर कुछ आश्चर्य हुआ। किसी अंग्रेज़ स्त्री से मिलने में मुझे क्या आपत्ति हो सकती थी। मि. रहमान शायद समझते थे कि काँग्रेस वाले अंग्रेज़ों को अपना दुश्मन समझते हैं, इसलिए शायद मुझे किसी अंग्रेज़-स्त्री से मिलना भी पसन्द न होगा। उन्हें यह पता नहीं था कि हमें किसी व्यक्ति-विशेष से द्वेष या घृणा नहीं है। यह तो महात्मा गान्धी के सिद्धान्त से बहुत दूर है। ख़ैर, मैंने कर्नल रहमान को कहा—''मुझे किसी अंग्रेज़ महिला से मिलने पर क्या आपत्ति हो सकती है? वह तो एक स्त्री होने के नाते मेरी बहन के समान है।''

दूसरे दिन प्रातःकाल ही मेरा वॉर्ड खुला। मैं बैठी हुई एक पुस्तक पढ़ रही थी कि इतने में मैंने देखा कि एक योरोपियन स्त्री और एक भारतीय महिला कर्नल रहमान के साथ-साथ अन्दर आ रही हैं। मैं अपनी बैरक से बाहर आयी। कर्नल रहमान ने परिचय देते हुए कहा—''यह मिसेज़ रहमान हैं। और दूसरी योरोपियन महिला मेरठ में किसी अंग्रेज़ इंजीनियर की स्त्री हैं।'' मिसेज़ रहमान ने मेरे साथ हाथ मिलाते ही पहला प्रश्न यह किया, ''क्या आप अंग्रेज़ी जानती हैं?''

मैंने उत्तर दिया, "हाँ, कुछ।"

इतना सुनते ही मिसेज़ रहमान के चेहरे पर एक प्रसन्नता का-सा भाव अंकित हो गया। मानो अंग्रेज़ी जानना बड़े गौरव की बात है। उस समय मेरे मन में एक ग्लानि का भाव उत्पन्न हुआ कि ग़ुलाम देश में अंग्रेज़ी जानना भी एक महत्व की बात समझी जाती है।

ख़ैर, मैं उन्हें अपनी बैरक के अन्दर ले गयी, पर वहाँ मेरे पास सिवाय खाट के और बैठाने को था ही क्या। मैंने उनसे कहा कि आजकल मेरा घर और सब कुछ यही है। बैरक में मेरा बिस्तर लोहे की खाट पर बिछा हुआ था, पास ही एक मिट्टी के चबूतरे पर मेरा बक्स रखा था और उसके पास ही एक छोटा-सा बेंत का बक्स था, जिसमें मैं खाने का सामान रखती थी। बस, यही मेरी गृहस्थी थी। पास के दूसरे चबूतरों पर 'सी क्लास' की स्त्रियों के कम्बल और चटाइयाँ पड़ी हुई थीं। अन्दर घुसते ही मिसेज़ रहमान यह कह कर बाहर निकल आयीं—'Oh! This is very dirty!' (अरे, यह तो बहुत गन्दा है।)

ठीक ही था, जिन लोगों की घुड़सालें भी उस बैरक से अच्छी हों, वे उसमें ठहरना क्यों पसन्द करतीं। फिर वे तो सुपरिण्टेण्डेण्ट जेल की स्त्री की हैसियत से वहाँ पर गयी थीं।

मैंने उनसे कहा कि मेरे पास तो सिवा उसके और कोई बिठाने की चीज़ नहीं है, इस पर जेलर ने एक जमादार को इशारा किया। बाहर से एक कुर्सी और बेंच आ गयी। इसके बाद मिसेज़ रहमान ने मुझ से पूछा कि—"आप जेल में कब से है?"

मैंने कहा—"18 जुलाई से।"

उन्होंने पूछा—"आप मेरठ में क्या थीं?"

उनका प्रश्न विचित्र-सा था। मैं समझ न सकी, मैंने उनसे पूछा कि आप का क्या मतलब है? फिर मिसेज़ रहमान ने कहा कि—"क्या आप लीडर थीं?"

मैंने उत्तर में कहा कि मैं काँग्रेस का काम करने वाली बहुत-सी बहनों में एक हूँ। मैं अपने भाइयों को विदेशी कपड़े छोड़ने और नशीली वस्तुओं का परहेज़ करने के लिए कहती थी। उसी अपराध में मैं जेल में डाली गयी हूँ। इतने में उनकी दृष्टि मेरी साड़ी पर पड़ी। उसे दिखा कर वे उस दूसरी योरोपियन महिला से कहने लगीं—'This is khaddar.' (यह खद्दर है।)

मैंने उनसे कहा कि आप भी खद्दर क्यों नहीं पहनतीं? मिसेज़ रहमान ने उसका कोई उत्तर नहीं दिया, फिर वे मुझसे पूछने लगी कि आप मेरठ में किस जगह रहती थीं? मैंने इसका साधारण उत्तर दे कर फिर उनसे कहा कि–''आप भी हिन्दुस्तानी हैं, आप काँग्रेस के काम में भाग क्यों नहीं लेतीं?''

मिसेज़ रहमान ने उत्तर दिया–''मैं कैसे ले सकती हूँ, मेरे पति तो सरकारी नौकर हैं।''

मैंने फिर कहा–''इससे क्या; इसी मेरठ में कई ऐसी स्त्रियाँ हैं जिनके पति सरकारी नौकर हैं पर वे हमारी मदद करती है। मुल्क को मदद पहुँचाने के बहुत-से तरीक़े हो सकते हैं।''

शायद मिसेज़ रहमान को मरी यह बात पसन्द न आयी और वे अधिक देर मेरे पास न रुकीं। अगले दिन डॉक्टर साहब जो मुझे दवा देने आते थे मुझसे पूछने लगे कि आपने मिसेज़ रहमान से क्या कहा था? मैंने कहा कि आप क्यों पूछते हैं, तो वे कहने लगे कि कर्नल रहमान कह रहे थे आपने उनसे खद्दर पहनने ओर काँग्रेस की मदद करने को कहा था। मैंने उत्तर दिया, ''बेशक मैंने कहा था, इसमें हर्ज क्या है?''

जिस मुलाक़ात का वर्णन मैंने ऊपर किया है, वह एक ढंग की थी। और ठीक उससे दूसरे ढंग की मुलाक़ात वह थी जो एक आइरिश योरोपियन महिला ने उसके कुछ दिन बाद मेरे साथ की। ऊपर की मुलाक़ात में मेरी एक हिन्दुस्तानी बहन थी, पर वह सहानुभूति के कारण मिलने नहीं आयी थी, उसे मेरे सुख-दुःख से मतलब न था, उसके लिए तो एक राजनैतिक महिला को क़ैदी के रूप में देखना एक तमाशे की चीज़ थी। परन्तु जो आइरिश महिला मुझ से मिलने आयी, उसके हृदय में सहानुभूति और प्रेम था, वह जेल की क़ैदिन का तमाशा देखने नहीं आयी थी, बल्कि वह उर्मिला से मिलने आयी थी।

उन दिनों मुझे ज्वर रहा करता था। उस भद्र महिला के आने की सूचना मुझे पहले से न दी गयी थी। मैं अपने बिस्तर पर लेटी हुई थी। एक साथ द्वार खटका। मैंने देखा कि सुपरिण्टेण्डेण्ट के साथ एक योरोपियन महिला आ रही है। मैं उन्हें देख कर आनन्द से उछल पड़ी। वे मेरी पूर्व-परिचित, मेरठ कॉलेज के प्रिन्सिपल की पत्नी श्रीमती ओडॉनल थीं। उन्होंने बड़े प्रेम से मेरे पास आ कर

हाथ मिलाया। मेरे सामने फिर वही चिन्ता उपस्थित हुई कि उन्हें कहाँ बिठाऊँ, पर वे शीघ्र ही मेरी कठिनाई समझ गयीं और कहने लगीं कि यह कोई तुम्हारा घर तो नहीं है, तुम संकोच क्यों करती हो?

फिर हम दोनों उसी बिस्तर पर साथ-साथ बैठ गयीं। कितने प्रेम से उन्होंने मेरे साथ बातें कीं, मेरे स्वास्थ्य का, रहन-सहन का समाचार पूछती रहीं। उनके प्रेम और सहानुभूति के कारण मुझे ऐसा प्रतीत हो रहा था कि मानो मेरी सारी बीमारी भागी जा रही हो। बैरक में मच्छर बहुत थे, और वे लगातार हम दोनों पर आक्रमण कर रहे थे, पर वे उसे सहती रहीं। फिर मुझसे पूछने लगीं–'यहाँ मच्छर तो बहुत हैं?"

मैंने कहा–"यह तो आप देख ही रही हैं। मच्छरों की वजह से मेरे हाथ पक गये हैं और ज्वर आता है।"

उन्होंने पूछा–"इसका सबब क्या है?"

मैंने कहा–"यहाँ आठवें दिन लिपाई होती है। जो मिट्टी लायी जाती है, वह बहुत गन्दी और बदबूदार होती है, शायद वह पास के गन्दे नाले से लायी जाती है। वस्तुतः मच्छरों का कारण वह मिट्टी ही थी। जव वह सूखी होती थी तभी उस पर मच्छर और मक्खियाँ उड़ने लगती थीं। एक-एक इंच लम्बे वे उस मिट्टी के अन्दर रहते थे। वही मिट्टी गोबर डाल कर लिपाई के काम में लायी जाती थी। जब मुझे ज्वर आने लगा तो मैंने कई बार प्रार्थना की कि उस मिट्टी से लिपाई न की जाये। परन्तु मेरी प्रार्थना व्यर्थ ही गयी। मैंने घर से मच्छरदानी भी मँगायी, पर वह खद्दर की थी, इसलिए हवा बन्द होने के कारण मैं उससे कोई लाभ न उठा सकी। मेरा ऐसा ख़याल है कि जेल में जाने वाले क़ैदियों को एक विशेष कष्ट मच्छरों का रहता है। मच्छर, क़ैदियों को जेल से डरा कर, सरकार की बड़ी सेवा करते हैं।

मैं ऊपर श्रीमती ओडॉनल का ज़िक्र कर रही थी, बहुत देर तक मैं उनके साथ बातें करती रही। उनके चले जाने पर मुझे कुछ क्षोभ-सा हुआ। उनकी इस प्रेमपूर्ण मुलाक़ात की स्मृति मेरे हृदय-पट पर चिरकाल तक अंकित रहेगी।

12

एकान्त-जीवन का अन्त

यद्यपि दो-तीन क़ैदी स्त्रियाँ मेरे जेल के आने के दिन से सदा ही फ़ीमेल-वॉर्ड में बनी रहीं, पर उनका होना या न होना मेरे लिए बराबर था। वे उस श्रेणी में आयी थीं, जिनके साथ मेरा कोई सहचार नहीं हो सकता था। मेरा ख़याल है कि यदि मैं ग्रामीण अपढ़ स्त्रियों के बीच रख दी जाती तो मैं उनमें भी मिल जाती और उनके साथ भी मुझे कुछ-न-कुछ संगति का स्वाद प्राप्त हो जाता। पर वे स्त्रियाँ जिनके साथ मुझे जेल में रहना पड़ा, उस दर्जे की थीं जैसी कि हमें बाहर कभी ही देखने को मिलती होंगी। ख़ून और चोरी व इसी तरह के दूसरे अपराधों में वे पकड़ कर आयी थीं। उनसे मुझे इतनी घृणा नहीं थी जितना कि डर लगता था। उनकी संगति की अपेक्षा यही अच्छा था कि मैं एकान्त जीवन व्यतीत करूँ। जेल में आने के दिन से लगातार पौने तीन महीने तक मेरा जेल-जीवन तनहाई का जीवन था। साधारणतया क़ैदियों को कोई बड़ा अपराध करने पर तनहाई की सज़ा मिलती है पर मुझे तो लगातार तनहाई मिली हुई थी। मेरी हालत किसी अंश में रॉबिन्सन क्रूसो के समान हो रही थी और कभी-कभी उसी के शब्दों में सोचा करती थी कि 'इस अपनी जेल-कोठरी में मेरा अखण्ड राज्य है।'

एक आशा थी जो मुझे जिला रही थी और जो मेरी सान्त्वना थी—मेरी बाहर की बहनें आज नहीं तो कल आ ही जायेंगी। पर जेल में एक सप्ताह नहीं, एक महीना और फिर दो महीने बीत गये, पर मैं अपनी कोठरी में अकेली ही रही! यह बात नहीं थी कि मेरे पीछे मेरी बहनों ने काम ढीला कर दिया हो; काम पूरे ज़ोर पर था, पर सरकार ने इरादा ही बदल दिया। मेरे पकड़ने पर जो कुछ परिणाम निकला उसको देखते हुए बुद्धिमत्ता भी यही थी कि आगे किसी को

न छेड़ा जाये, नहीं तो मेरे पकड़ने के अगले दिन ही मेरे साथ काम करने वाली बहनों ने जो कुछ किया था, वह मेरठ-जेल की सारी फ़ीमेल वॉर्ड को भरने के लिए काफ़ी था। पर सरकार मौन साध गयी। मैं जिस दिन पकड़ी गयी थी, उससे पहले दिन ही मैंने अपने भाषण में कहा था, "जेल न सिडीशन से मिलती है, न शराब की पिकेटिंग से, और न कपड़े के बॉयकॉट कराने से; वह तो केवल भाग्य से मिलती है।" मैं स्वयं जेल आने के दिन से तीन महीने पूर्व से लगातार वही काम कर रही थी। न जाने कितने व्याख्यान दिये और कितने दिन पिकेटिंग में लगाये, पर कभी कुछ न हुआ। पर जब शुभ मुहूर्त आया तो मुझे इस बात पर पकड़ लिया गया कि मैंने कॉलेज के विद्यार्थियों से कहा था कि तुम वॉलण्टियर बनो। और सचमुच जब मैजिस्ट्रेट ने मुझ से पूछा, "क्या तुमने विद्यार्थियों को पिकेटिंग करने के लिए कहा था।" तो मुझे हँसी आयी, मैंने मजिस्ट्रेट को कहा कि मैंने तो इससे बहुत अधिक कहा था। ऐसी हालत में किसी का पकड़ा या न पकड़ा जाना केवल सरकार की नीति पर निर्भर था। पर जो पकड़े जाते थे, वे यह सोच कर सन्तोष कर लेते थे कि हमारी क़ीमत सरकार ने लगा दी है। ख़ैर, ऐसी हालत में यदि दूसरी बहनें बहुत दिन जेल में नहीं आयीं तो इसे या तो मेरी बदनसीबी कहना चाहिए या उनकी ही।

अन्ततः 12 अक्टूबर को मेरे एकान्त-जीवन का अन्त हो गया। मेरे जेल वाले घर में मेरी राजनैतिक कार्यक्षेत्र की सहयोगिनी तीन बहनें मेहमान बन कर आ गयीं। इनमें से दो बहनें तो बॉयकॉट में मेरी सहयोगिनी श्रीमती प्रकाशवती और श्रीमती विद्यावती जी थीं, और तीसरी बहन मेरठ के महिला चरखा संघ की मन्त्रिणी श्रीमती कमलादेवी चौधरानी थीं। मुझे उस दिन कितना हर्ष हुआ होगा, इसका अनुमान करना पाठकों के लिए कठिन होगा। वृक्ष की शीतल छाया का स्वाद वही जानता है, जो कड़कती हुई धूप में दूर से चल कर आया हो। आग की गर्मी का आनन्द उसे ही मिलता है, जो पूस की सर्दी में नंगा पड़ा हुआ अकड़ गया हो। उन बहनों का आना मेरे लिए क्या था? मानो चिर-कंगाल को इकट्ठी धनराशि मिल गयी हो। वह दिन मेरे लिए एक विशेष उत्सव का दिन था। यहाँ तक कि जेल के लोगों ने मुझे बधाई भेजी कि आज से आपकी तनहाई समाप्त होती है।

जेल के अधिकारी ही क्या जो ऐसे मौक़े पर अपनी भलमनसाहत का स्वाँग न दिखायें। न जाने किस-किस मतलब से जेलर वहाँ पहुँचे ओर कहने लगे—"नयी

आयी हुई स्त्रियों की अभी कोई क्लास तय नहीं हुई है, इसलिए क़ायदे के मुताबिक़ उनके साथ 'सी' क्लास का सलूक़ होना चाहिए, पर लिहाज़ के कारण मैं उनके लिए भी कच्चा खाना भिजवाये देता हूँ जिसमें उन्हें कोई तकलीफ़ न हो।"

यहाँ यह बतला देना आवश्यक है कि साधारणतया किसी क़ैदी की क्लास, सज़ा के समय बतलायी जाती थी। इसलिए मुक़दमे का फ़ैसला होने तक कोई क्लास न होती थी। पर पुलिस के लोगों ने यह समझ कर कि यदि स्त्रियों के साथ बुरा सलूक़ हुआ तो बारूद में चिनगारी लग जायगी, जनता भड़क उठेगी, जेल में आने वाली स्त्रियों के वॉरण्ट के साथ ही फ़ैसला होने तक के लिए 'ए' क्लास निश्चित कर दी थी। शायद जेलर को इस बात का पता न था या जान-बूझ कर वे इस बात को उड़ाना चाहते थे। विद्यावती जी ने कहा—"हमारी क्लास निश्चित हो चुकी है। कृपा करके हमारे लिए खाटों का इन्तजाम कर दीजिए।"

जेलर—"मैं क्या इन्तज़ाम करूँ?"

विद्यावती जी—"मेरी खाट तो 'ए' क्लास पुरुष-वॉर्ड में कहीं पड़ी होगी। क्योंकि जब मेरे पति जेल आये थे तो घर से खाट भिजवायी गयी थी। अब उनकी बदली हो गयी है, वह ख़ाली होगी। और दूसरी बहनों के लिए घर से खाट मँगा लीजिए।"

जेलर—"सी क्लास वालों को खाट नहीं मिलती।" इतना कहता हुआ चला गया। परन्तु अन्ततः कुछ तंग करने के बाद खाटों का प्रबन्ध हो गया।

इसके बाद नयी आयी हुई स्त्रियों का नियमपूर्वक मुलाहिज़ा करने के लिए सुपरिण्टेण्डेण्ट-जेल कर्नल रहमान ने फ़ीमेल वॉर्ड में प्रवेश किया। हम लोग रसोई में लगी हुई थीं। जमादारिन के आवाज़ देने पर बाहर निकल आयीं। सुपरिण्टेण्डेण्ट ने सब से नाम-धाम आदि पूछने शुरू किये। विद्यावतीजी और प्रकाशवती जी से पूछ कर, कमला जी से भी वही प्रश्न दुहराये—

सुप.—"आपके पति का नाम?"

कमला जी—"डॉक्टर चौधरी।"

सुप.—"क्या आप बंगाली हैं?"

कमला जी—"नहीं! हम लखनऊ के रहने वाले हैं।"

सुप.—"चौधरी साहब ने डॉक्टरी कहाँ से पास की?"

कमला जी—"कलकत्ते से।"

सुप.—अगर आप बंगाली नहीं हैं तो कलकत्ते से क्यों की; लखनऊ से क्यों नहीं की?''

कमला जी—''यह तो आप उनसे ही पूछिए।''

अन्तिम उत्तर से सुपरिण्टेण्डेण्ट की त्योरियाँ चढ़ गयी। 'उनसे ही पूछिए' इन शब्दों में जेल के नवाब साहब को कुछ अपमान की गन्ध आने लगी। वहाँ से तो चले गये, परन्तु उनका क्रोध भड़क उठा। इसका बदला लिये बिना कैसे रह सकते थे। श्रीमती कमला देवी की मुलाक़ात बन्द कर दी गयी। तीन-चार दिन बाद बड़ी मुश्किल से इजाज़त मिली। इस पर कोई टीका-टिप्पणी व्यर्थ है। जेल में आयी हुई एक स्त्री के सीधे-सादे यथोचित उत्तर में अपनी मानसिक कमज़ोरी के कारण अपमान की गन्ध आ जाने से या आदर की कमी का अनुभव करने के कारण नाराज़ हो कर एक आश्रित स्त्री के प्रति बदला लेने की इच्छा को मनुष्य-मनोभावों की किस गिनती में रखा जाय, इसका उत्तर शायद मनोविज्ञान-शास्त्री ही दे सकेंगे।

12 अक्टूबर के बाद जेल का मेरा सूना घर आबाद हो गया। उसमें भी झण्डे का गान गूँजने लगा, उसमें भी चहल-पहल रहने लगी। केवल कभी-कभी मेरे हृदय में एक हल्की-सी वेदना होती थी कि मैं अपने एकान्त-वास के एकमात्र साथी पेड़ और पक्षियों को भूलती जा रही थी।

13

जेल का भोजन

जेल में यों तो तीनों तरह के क़ैदियों को वहीं का भोजन मिलता है। पर 'ए' क्लास वाले अपने घर से भी मँगा कर खा सकते है। जेल मैनुएल में दिया गया है कि 'ए' क्लास के क़ैदी अपना भोजन घर से 'सप्लीमेन्ट' (पूरा) कर सकते हैं। 'सप्लीमेंट' का अर्थ लगाना जेल के अधिकारियों पर निर्भर होता है। कभी-कभी वे कहते हैं कि केवल फल लिये जा सकते हैं और कभी-कभी सभी अधिक चीज़ें भी ले ली जाती हैं। जब मैं जेल गयी ही थी, लगभग एक सप्ताह तक मुझे जेल में पका हुआ भोजन भेज दिया जाता था; अनुकूल न पड़ने के कारण उसके बाद मैंने स्वयं खाना पकाने की आज्ञा प्राप्त कर ली। तब मुझे ज्ञात हुआ कि मुझे किस हिसाब से रोज़ खाना दिया जाता है।

मुझे कहा गया कि आपकी सादी क़ैद है, जेल में 'ए' क्लास की सादी क़ैदवाले को छः आना रोज़ के हिसाब से खाना दिया जाता है, और सख़्त क़ैदवाले को आठ आने के हिसाब से। मुझ दोनों समय का इकट्ठा कच्चा सामान तोल कर दिया जाने लगा। वह इस प्रकार था–

पाँच छटाँक दूध।

तीन तोले चावल–(बाद में इनकी मात्रा ४ तोले हो गयी)।

एक छटाँक आलू–जो संख्या में अधिकतर एक होता था।

दो छटाँक दाल।

आधी छटाँक बूरा (मीठा)।

सवा सेर लकड़ी।

छः छटाँक आटा।

चौथाई छटाँक नमक।

आधा छटाँक मिर्च-मसाला।

आधा तोला चाय।

आधा छटाँक घी।

बाद में दो छटाँक सूजी भी मिलने लगी। पर यह समझ में नहीं आया कि यह क्यों दी जाती थी। पूछने पर पता चला कि ऊपर से कोई आर्डर आया है। इसी हिसाब से 'बी' क्लास में भी खाना जाया करता था। यदि कोई स्वास्थ्य ख़राब हो जाने की वजह से खाना बन्द कर दे तो डॉक्टर की आज्ञा से उसी हिसाब से खाने के बदले दूध या और चीज़ें मिलने लगती थीं।

सज़ा के अन्तिम दो मासों में जब मेरा स्वास्थ्य ख़राब था तब ऊपर के सामान के बदले निम्न चीज़ें मिलने लगीं–

तीन पाव दूध।

आधा औंस मक्खन।

एक छटाँक आलू।

एक डबल रोटी।

'सी' क्लास वालों का भोजन बहुत ज़्यादा बुरा होता था। उन्हें घी की जगह तेल मिलता था। रोटियाँ आधी जली, आधी कच्ची रहती थीं। आटे में रेत की तो कुछ हद ही नहीं होती थी। कभी-कभी हम लोग शाम को दो रोटी और सब्ज़ी 'सी' क्लास वालों की ले लिया करती थीं। उनके विषय में मैं तो केवल इतना कह सकती हूँ कि सिवा खाने वाले के, दूसरा कोई भी अनुमान नहीं कर सकता। शाक में प्रायः तेल कच्चा ही डाल दिया जाता था। मिर्चें इतनी होती थीं कि खाया ही न जा सके; रोटी और सब्ज़ी दोनों में ही रेत होती थी। यों तो जेल डॉक्टर को आज्ञा होती थी कि वह सब्ज़ी चढ़ने के समय अपनी आँखों से सब देखे, पर ऐसा कभी होता ही न था। डॉक्टर साहब ने कम्पाउण्डर पर डाल दिया; सैकड़ों क़ैदी और बेचारा एक कम्पाउण्डर; वह दवाई बाँटे या खाना पकता देखे। फल यह होता था कि दोनों ही बातें रह जाती थीं; न रोगियों को ठीक औषधि ही मिलती और न खाना ही सफ़ाई से बनता था। हाँ, जब कोई अफ़सर जेल-निरीक्षण के लिए आता था तब डॉक्टर साहब जा कर देख आते थे।

नियमानुसार जेल के बाग़ में जो सब्ज़ी पैदा हो, वह जेल के क़ैदियों को मिलनी चाहिए, पर जेल के क़ैदियों की, विशेषकर 'सी' क्लास वालों की,

शिकायत थी कि बाग़ में पैदा हुई सब्ज़ी जेल के कर्मचारियों के भेंट हो जाती थी। मैं नहीं कह सकती कि यह बात कहाँ तक ठीक थी, पर कहा जाता था कि जब कभी 'सी' क्लास में गोभी के फूल बनने को जाते तो रसोई-घर तक पहुँचते-पहुँचते फूलों की जगह पत्ते ही रह जाते थे, और मोटे-मोटे डण्ठल गोभी के नाम से क़ैदियों को खाने के लिए मिलते थे। कोई भी दाल बने, सभी का रंग काला होता था। रोटियाँ जली और कच्ची; दोनों ही बातें एक साथ होती थीं। वे पकी और जली होने पर भी गल जाती थीं। सब्ज़ी में कच्चा तेल डालने का कारण शायद यह था कि यदि आरम्भ में तेल डाला जाये तो मिक़दार के मुताबिक़ पूरा डालना पड़ता है और अगर सारा डालना पड़े तो कई लोगों की रोज़ की मालिश रह जाये और तेल से होने वाले दूसरे कार्य कैसे हो सकें। इसलिए तेल अन्त में डाला जाता है, वह कच्चा तो रहता है, पर दीखता अधिक है। तीसरी बात रोटी में रेत होने की थी, उसका कारण तो और भी स्पष्ट है। प्रत्येक क़ैदी को तोल कर रोटी दी जाती है; प्रायः हिसाब से पाँच ही रोटियाँ प्रत्येक के हिस्से में पड़ती हैं। जो लोग साधारण काम करते हैं, उनकी बात जाने दो, पर जिन्हें सोलह-सोलह सेर आटा रोज़ पीसने को मिलता हो, उनका पेट इन हलकी-हल्की पाँच रोटियों से कैसे भर सकता था, इसलिए वे लोग भूख की ज्वाला को शान्त करने के लिए पीसते समय कच्चा आटा खा लेते हैं, पर उन्हें पीस कर वापस देते समय पूरा आटा देना होता है, उसको पूरा करने के लिए वे रेत मिला देते हैं। फिर इसी नुस्ख़े को वॉर्डर और जेल के सिपाही भी काम में ला सकते हैं। जितना आटा लेना हुआ, उतनी ही रेत डाल कर तोल पूरी कर दी, इस प्रकार जेल की रोटियों में रेत होने की आम शिकायत बनी रहती है। जेल की सब्ज़ी, जिसे 'भुजिया' कहा जाता है, अपने ढंग की अनूठी चीज़ होती है, उसका स्वाद चखने से ही ताल्लुक़ रखता है, वह लेखनी का विषय नहीं।

14

जेल में श्रेणी भेद

अमर शहीद प्रातः स्मरणीय श्री यतीन्द्रदास के अनुपम बलिदान का यह फल हुआ था कि एक बार पत्थर-हृदय भारत सरकार का भी ध्यान इस ओर आकर्षित हुआ कि जेल में सड़ने वाले राजनैतिक क़ैदियों के साथ पशुओं का-सा व्यवहार न हो। बहुत-सी जाँच-पड़ताल होने के बाद यह फ़ैसला हुआ कि साधारण क़ैदियों के अतिरिक्त अच्छी स्थिति रखने वाले राजनैतिक क़ैदियों को 'ए' और 'बी' क्लास में रखा जाये। उपर्युक्त दोनों क्लासों में क़ैदियों को कुछ सुविधाएँ देने के लिए कुछ नियम भी बना दिये गये। अब इतने दिन के अनुभव के पश्चात कहा जा सकता है कि इसमें भी भेद का कितना दुष्परिणाम हुआ है। और सरकारी कर्मचारियों ने इस श्रेणी के द्वारा अपनी फूट डालने वाली नीति से अच्छी तरह काम लिया है।

यह कहने की आवश्यकता नहीं कि पिछले सत्याग्रह संग्राम के दिनों में कई बार अत्यन्त प्रतिष्ठित लोगों की 'बी' क्लास ही नहीं 'सी' क्लास क़ैद दी गयी। दर्जनों इसके उदाहरण दिये जा सकते हैं। कई अफ़सरों ने समझा था कि इस प्रकार अनुचित श्रेणी भेद करने से सत्याग्रहियों के हृदयों में क्षोभ उत्पन्न होगा। इतना ही नहीं, जेल के अन्दर 'सी' क्लास के सत्याग्रहियों को बार-बार भड़काया जाता था कि तुम लोग 'सी' क्लास में सड़ रहे हो, तुम्हारे लीडर 'ए' और 'बी' क्लास में मौज उड़ाते है। कई बार अनेक जेलों में 'ए' और 'बी' क्लास के सत्याग्रहियों ने केवल इस दृष्टि से कि वे भी 'सी' क्लास वालों के कष्टों का अनुभव कर सकें, 'सी' क्लास में अपने को बदलवाने के लिए प्रार्थना-पत्र दिये,

परन्तु इन प्रार्थना-पत्रों को स्वीकार करना भी जेल के अधिकारियों के हाथ में ही होता था और प्रायः ऐसे प्रार्थना-पत्र स्वीकार नहीं किये जाते थे।

साथ ही यह समझ लेना चाहिए कि 'ए' क्लास और 'बी' क्लास वालों को वे सब सुविधाएँ प्राप्त थीं जो उन्हें जेल मैनुएल के अनुसार मिलनी चाहिएँ, पर उन सुविधाओं का देना सर्वथा जेल के कर्मचारियों पर निर्भर होता था, किन्हीं जेलों में पर्याप्त सुविधाएँ और किन्हीं में बहुत कम। और कभी सुविधाएँ मिल भी गयीं तो कभी बन्द कर दी गयीं।

जब मैं पहले जेल में पहुँची तो मैंने लिखने के लिए काग़ज़ माँगा। 'ए' क्लास वालों को लिखने के लिए काग़ज़ मिल सकता है, पर मुझे बहुत दिन तक बहुत-सा झगड़ा-बखेड़ा होने के बाद काग़ज़ मिला, एक बार तो जेलर ने मुझे यही सूचना भेज दी कि महीने में केवल दो बार ख़त लिखने के लिए काग़ज़ मिलेगा और कोई काग़ज़ नहीं मिल सकता। परन्तु अन्त में मुझे लिखने के लिए एक कापी दे दी गयी।

पर साथ ही यह भी उचित ही होगा यदि मैं उस सुविधा का भी उल्लेख कर दूँ जो जेल के सुपरिण्टेण्डेण्ट कर्नल रहमान ने मुझे दी थी। जुलाई और अगस्त में मेरठ की गरमी का अनुमान किया जा सकता है उन दिनों में मुझे बैरक के अन्दर बन्द कमरे में सोना पड़ता था, सुपरिण्टेण्डेण्ट को मेरे ऊपर दया आ गयी, उन्होंने मुझे घर से मिट्टी के तेल से चलने वाले पंखे को मँगाने की आज्ञा दे दी, यही एक विशेष कृपा का उदाहरण है जो मुझे अपने जेल-जीवन में प्राप्त हुई। यद्यपि उस पंखे से मुझे कोई लाभ नहीं हुआ; क्योंकि उसकी आवाज़ और बदबू से नींद में बाधा पड़ती थी और वह कभी अकस्मात बन्द भी हो जाता था, इसलिए मुझे उसका उपयोग बन्द ही करना पड़ा।

'ए' क्लास में एक और भी कठिनता होती थी। अतः हरेक चीज़ के लिए कह दिया जाता था कि अपने घर से मँगा लो, हम लोगों के लैम्पों में पर्याप्त तेल नहीं भरा जाता था।

हमारी बैरक में तो एक और भी विशेष कष्ट था कि जिस बैरक में हम लोग रहती थीं, उसमें कबूतरों के भी अनेक घर बने हुए थे। जिन लोगों ने 'सी' क्लास की बैरकें देखी हैं, वे हमारी बैरक का अन्दाज़ा कर सकते हैं, ऐसी बैरकों में घोंसला बनाने के बहुत स्थान रहते हैं। ऊपर शहतीरों और कड़ियों पर कबूतरों के घोंसले और ठीक उनके नीचे हमारे बिस्तर रहते थे। बैठने को कोई

और जगह तो थी ही नहीं, बस हर समय हम लोगों को कबूतरों की बीटों का उपहार मिलता था। कभी किसी का घोंसला गिर पड़ा तो नीचे या तो हम और या हमारा बिस्तर तमाम तिनकों और फूटे हुए अण्डों से ख़राब हो जाता था। कभी तो ठीक सिर के ऊपर बीट आ-आ कर गिरती थीं। हम लोगों के सामान में से रज़ाई से ले कर पहनने तक के कपड़ों में से कोई चीज़ ऐसी न थी जिसे हमें बीट की वजह से धोना न पड़ा हो। हम लोग परेड के दिन सुपरिण्टेण्डेग्ट से बराबर कहते थे, पर कोई फल न हुआ। इसी बीच में एक बार कलेक्टर साहब भी बैरक देखने आये; मैंने उनको अपने कपड़े, जो उनके आने से शायद दो या तीन मिनट पहले ख़राब हुए थे, दिखाये। कलेक्टर ने मुझसे कहा—हम अगर जेल ख़र्च में कुछ गुंजायश देखेंगे तो छत पर टाट या चटाई लग जायेगी।

लेकिन मेरे बाद में भी जो बहनें वहाँ रहीं, और जब वह अपनी क़ैद के दिन समाप्त करके वापस आयीं तो मैंने उन से यही सुना कि छत पर चटाई आदि कुछ नहीं लगी। यह तो 'ए' और 'बी' क्लास के रहने वालों की हालत थी; इसी से अनुमान किया जा सकता है कि बेचारे 'सी' क्लास वालों का क्या हाल होता होगा। मेरठ डिस्ट्रिक्ट जेल में रहने वाले 'सी' क्लास के भाइयों की अवस्था को ठीक नहीं तो कुछ-न-कुछ मैं जानती हूँ। प्रत्येक छोटी माँग को पूरा करवाने के लिए भूख-हड़ताल की ज़रूरत होती थी। 'ए' और 'बी' क्लास वालों की भूख-हड़ताल तो कुछ फ़ायदेमन्द भी रहती थी, पर 'सी' क्लास में भूख-हड़ताल करना अपने मुँह से तनहाई या बेड़ी माँगना होता था।

मुझे याद, है कि गढ़मुक्तेश्वर के मेले पर, हर साल की तरह इस बार भी पच्चीस स्त्रियाँ मेले में से चोरी के सन्देह में पकड़ कर जेल में लायी गयी थीं; जेल के स्त्री वॉर्ड में एक ही पाख़ाना बना हुआ था; स्वभावतः उस में गन्दगी बढ़नी थी, मैंने जेलर साहब से कहा—मेरे लिए एक दूसरा प्रबन्ध करवा दीजिए। लगातार चार दिन जब कहते हुए हो गये और कोई प्रबन्ध न हुआ तब अन्त में तंग आ कर मैंने वॉर्डर के द्वारा जेलर साहब को कहलवाया—"आज ही शाम तक कुछ-न-कुछ प्रबन्ध करवा दें, नहीं तो मैं भूख-हड़ताल निश्चय ही कर दूँगी।" जिस के उत्तर में जेलर ने कहलवाया—"अगर आप ऐसा करेंगी, साहब आपको ट्रान्सफ़र कर देंगे।" मैंने कहा—"अच्छी बात है, मैं अभी से भूख-हड़ताल की सूचना देती हूँ।" जेलर को यक़ीन हो गया कि अवश्य भूख-हड़ताल होगी। इसलिए उसी शाम को नये पाख़ाने का प्रबन्ध करवा दिया गया।

'ए' क्लास में होने का एक मात्र लाभ जो मुझे पता लगा सिर्फ़ यह था कि मैं महीने में दो बार पत्र लिख सकती थी और दो बार मेरी मिलायी होती थी। ख़ासकर आरम्भ के तीन महीनों में जब मैं अकेली थी, मेरे लिए ये दोनों बातें अधिक महत्वपूर्ण थीं।

सब बातों को देखते हुए मेरी यह निश्चित सम्मति है कि यह श्रेणी भेद हमारे लिए अत्यन्त हानिकारक और नैतिक दृष्टि से भी अनुचित है। शिक्षित लोगों के 'ए' और 'बी' क्लास में चले जाने के कारण 'सी' क्लास के क़ैदियों के कष्ट की कोई सीमा नहीं रहती और कई बार उनको, जैसा कि ऊपर कहा गया है भड़काया भी जाता है। यदि ऐसी हालत में उनमें असन्तोष हो जाय तो कोई आश्चर्य नहीं।

कहा जाता है कि जो लोग बाहर भिन्न-भिन्न स्थिति में रहते हैं, यदि उन्हें जेल के अन्दर एक ही ढंग से रहना पड़े तो कितनी बड़ी कठिनता होगी। यदि 'ए' और 'बी' क्लास तोड़ दी जाये तो क्या ऊँची स्थिति में आराम से रहने वाले लोग 'सी' क्लास में रह सकेंगे? इन बातों का उत्तर तो स्पष्ट ही है। यदि सब लोग एक साथ ही रखे जायेंगे तो 'सी' क्लास वालों की दशा अब से बहुत उत्तम होगी। उन के साथ जो पशुवत व्यवहार किया जाता है, वह असम्भव हो जायेगा। एक भाव है जो कई बार मेरे मन में आता रहा है। काँग्रेस ऐसे स्वराज्य की कल्पना कर रही है जिसमें अमीर-ग़रीब का भेद-भाव बहुत हद तक मिट जायेगा जिस में अमीर-ग़रीब दोनों को खाने-पीने, रहने-सहने की समान सुविधाएँ प्राप्त होंगी। यदि जेल को स्वराज्य का मार्ग समझते हैं तो क्या यह उचित नहीं कि जेल में हम भाई-भाई की इस समानता की एक झलक देख सकें?

यह आवश्यक है कि काँग्रेस की ओर से श्रेणी-भेद तोड़ने के लिए ज़बर्दस्त आन्दोलन किया जाये।

15

जेल से मेरी मुक्ति

रोज़ सुनती थी कि, ज्वर आने के कारण मुझे शीघ्र छोड़ दिया जायेगा। पाँच महीने भी व्यतीत हो चुके थे। और यह भी सुना था, कि निवाड़ बुनने के कारण कुछ दिन की छूट भी मिलेगी, पर किस दिन छोड़ा जायेगा, इसका मुझे कुछ पता न था। एक दिन परेड के समय प्रातः ही मेरा हिस्टरी टिकट[1] माँगा गया। मैंने देखा उस पर मेरी रिहाई की तारीख़ दो जनवरी पड़ी हुई थी। वह काट कर ६ जनवरी कर दी गयी।

कौन ऐसा होगा, जिसे अपने घर जाने की आकांक्षा न हो, और अपने मित्र तथा सम्बधियों से मिलने की इच्छा न हो। मनुष्य का स्वभाव है कि वह कभी एक ही अवस्था में सन्तुष्ट नहीं रहता, अच्छी-से-अच्छी जगह में भी लगातार रह चुकने के बाद एक दिन ऐसा समय आता ही है जब उसी स्थान को छोड़ने के लिए व्याकुल होने लगता है और फिर अपना घर चाहे वह कितना भी बुरा हो, एक टूटा-फूटा झोंपड़ा ही हो, किसी महल में रहते हुए भी मनुष्य उसके लिए पागल हो उठता है। यह कहावत है –East or West, home is the best, उन दिनों यह मुहावरा मुझे इतना पसन्द था कि मैंने अपने तकिये के ग़िलाफ़ के एक कोने में भी इसे काढ़ ही डाला। मेरे सामने तो उस समय दुनिया की सबसे ज़्यादा

1. हरेक क़ैदी का एक 'हिस्टरी टिकट उसकी जेल-जीवन-चर्या के रूप में रखा जाता है जिसमें उनके काम का, इनाम का, दण्ड और बीमारी आदि का हाल अंकित किया जाता है।

ख़ूबसूरत और प्यारी चीज़ों में मेरा घर था। एक देवता के मन्दिर की तरह मैं उसके दर्शन के लिए उत्सुक होने लगी। मैं सोचती कि मेरे छूटने के समय मुझे कैसे बुलाया जायेगा। मेरे मित्र, मेरे सम्बन्धी, द्वार पर मेरी प्रतीक्षा करते होंगे, मैं द्वार पर जाऊँगी, इस जेल की चाहारदीवारी के बाहर! आह, तब मेरे साथ कोई सिपाही न होगा! मैं सड़कों पर बिना लाल पगड़ी वाले रक्षकों के घूम सकूँगी।

कभी-कभी मैं सोचती कि मेरी हालत क्या उस चिड़िया से कुछ कम होगी जो पिंजरे के अन्दर बन्द है और फिर भी वह उसी पिंजरे में घूम-घूम कर अपने बाग़ का, उसी घोंसले का, जिसे उसने छोटे-छोटे तिनकों को कई दिन तक मुँह से उठा-उठा कर एक पेड़ की सूखी शाख पर बनाया था, मार्ग खोजा करती है, पर क्रूर व्याध उसे हर समय साँकल लगा कर अकेले छटपटाने के लिए छोड़ देता है, एस समय मुझे कवि इक़बाल का यह गीत याद आता था–

आता है याद मुझको गुज़रा हुआ ज़माना।
वो झाड़ियाँ चमन की, वो मेरा अशियाना।।
वो साथ सब के उड़ना, वो सैर आसमाँ की।
ठण्डी हवा के पीछे, वो तालियाँ बजाना।।
अरमान है ये जी में उड़ कर चमन में जाऊँ।
टहनी से घुल के बैठूँ, आज़ाद हो के गाऊँ।।
बेरी की शाख पर हो, वैसा ही फिर बसेरा।
उस उजड़े घोंसले को, फिर जाके मैं बसाऊँ।।

आख़िर वह दिन भी आया, लेकिन मैं बेख़बर थी, क्योंकि मुझे तो छः तारीख़ का इन्तज़ार था। पर उस दिन तो तीन ही तारीख़ थी, मैं ही क्यों शहर के लोग और यहाँ तक कि मेरे घर वाले भी इससे अनभिज्ञ थे।

बहन कमला जी बीमार थीं। कोई 9 बजे होंगे, हमारी बैरक के सामने धूप आ गयी थी, वहीं उनका बिस्तर बिछा कर मैंने उन्हें लिटाया ही था कि द्वार खटका। द्वार खोल कर जमादार ने अपने पुराने ढंग से कहा–"उर्मिला जी, चलिए।"

बीमार रहने की वजह से मैं सप्ताह में इसी दिन प्रायः इसी समय पर हस्पताल जाया करती थी। पर आज 11 दिन हो गये थे, मेरे कहने पर भी मुझे हस्पताल नहीं भेजा गया। मैंने समझा, वहीं के लिए बुला रहे हैं।

मैंने कहा–"जब मुझे तकलीफ़ थी, तब तो भेजा नहीं; आज मैं नहीं जाती। अब तो एक बार घर जाने के लिए ही बैरक से बाहर निकलूँगी।"

वॉर्डर ने कहा—"हाँ, घर के लिए ही तो बुला रहा हूँ।"

मुझे अपने कानों पर विश्वास न हुआ। मेरी बहनों ने एक साथ कहना शुरू किया—"लो आज तुमने हमारा साथ छोड़ दिया...."

वॉर्डर ने कहा, "जल्दी करिए, आपका नौकर दरवाज़े पर खड़ा है।"

मैं और भी हैरान हुई। क्या सारे घर में से मेरा नौकर ही मुझे लेने आया है? मैंने धड़कते हुए दिल के साथ उससे पूछा कि क्या और कोई नहीं आया? वॉर्डर ने कहा, कोई नहीं और वह नौकर भी तो आप के मैले कपड़े लेने आया था। उसे भी यह क्या पता था कि आज आप छूटेंगी। पर साहब ने कहा कि आप को आज ही छोड़ दिया जाये।

पूरे साढ़े पाँच मास जिस बैरक में, जिन दीवारों के भीतर व्यतीत किये थे, जहाँ आधी गर्मी, पूरी बरसात, और उसके बाद आधे जाड़े के दिन व्यतीत किये थे, वहाँ अब मुझे घड़ी भर भी खड़े होने की आज्ञा नहीं थी। मुझे पता नहीं किस तरह मेरा बिस्तर और बक्स बन्द हो गया। हाँ, मुझे याद है ठीक दस मिनट के अन्दर ही एक और व्यक्ति यही सन्देश देने मेरे पास आ पहुँचा। मेरी बहनों ने हँसते-हँसते मुझे विदा किया, मैं बैरक से बाहर द्वार तक आयी, सिपाही और वॉर्डरों से घिरा हुआ बड़ा लोहे का द्वार बन्द था। हाँ, बाहर मेरा नौकर गोवबर्धन खड़ा मेरी प्रतीक्षा कर रहा था।

वॉर्डर ने कहा "आप दफ़्तर में चलिए; साहब बुलाते हैं।" वॉर्डर के साथ मैं ऊपर दफ़्तर में पहुँची।

सुपरिण्टेण्डेण्ट ने पूछा—"क्या हाल है?"

मैंने कहा—"अच्छा है।"

सुपरिण्टेण्डेण्ट—"आज आप बाहर जायेगा?"

मैंने कहा—"जी हाँ। ख़ैर देखें, फिर कब इधर आना हो।"

आश्चर्य से सुपरिण्टेण्डेण्ट ने कहा—"क्या बोला, फिर आइएगा इधर जेल में?"

मैंने नीचे उतरते हुए कहा—"शायद...."

मैं नीचे चली आयी। मेरे साथ ही नायब जेलर भी उतर आया। मुझ से कह गया—"अभी यहीं ठहरै, सामान चेक होने के बाद आप को जाना होगा।" जेल के कर्मचारी आते और उधर से निकल जाते। लगभग एक घण्टा खड़े रहने के बाद तंग आ कर मैंने नायब जेलर से कहा —"अगर आप को अभी फ़ुरसत नहीं

तो मुझे फ़ीमेल वॉर्ड में भेज दिया जाये, जब ख़ाली होंगे तब देख लेना।'' मैं कह ही रही थी, तभी दफ़्तर काम ख़त्म करके सुपरिण्टेण्डेण्ट नीचे उतरे। मुझे इस तरह खड़े देख कर उन्होंने जेलर से कहा—''इन्हें जाने क्यों नहीं दिया जाता?'' जेलर ने कहा—''अभी इनका सामान देखा जायेगा।'' सुपरिण्टेण्डेण्ट ने पास पड़ी हुई एक कुर्सी की ओर इशारा कर के कहा—''आप यहाँ बैठ जाइए।'' इतना कह कर सुपरिण्टेण्डेण्ट तो चले गये। जेलर ने मेरा सामान अपने दफ़्तर में मँगा लिया। एक नम्बरदार ने मेरा बिस्तर खोला, दूसरे ने बॉक्स, प्रत्येक चीज़ को झाड़-झाड़ कर देखा। वहाँ था ही क्या जो नज़र आता। मेरे पास प्रोफ़ेसरजी और एक छोटी लड़की की तस्वीर थी। इसके अतिरिक्त जेलवालों के द्वारा आयी हुई प्रोफ़ेसरजी की चिट्ठियाँ थीं। वह सब चिट्ठियाँ और चित्र मेज़ पर रखवा लिये गये।

मेरे पास एक और कापी भी थी, जिस पर कभी मैं कुछ नोट करने योग्य बात मैं इसी कापी में नोट कर लेती थी। पर उसमें कोई ऐसा साहित्य न लिखा गया था, जो बाहर जाने लायक़ न हो। अधिकतर रवीन्द्रनाथ टैगौर के ही उद्धरण लिखे हुए थे, और वह भी शायद आठ-दस पृष्ठों से ज़्यादा न होंगे। अधिकतर उस कापी के पृष्ठ अर्ज़ी लिखने का काम देते थे, पर शायद मुझे तंग करने के लिए वह भी मेज़ पर रखवा ली गयी। पूरे एक घण्टे या उससे भी अधिक समय में मेरी तलाशी का खेल समाप्त हुआ। चित्र तो चुपचाप वापस कर दिये गये, पर पर्चों को देने से जेलर ने इनकार कर दिया, मैंने उसका कारण पूछा—तो जेलर ने कहा—आप को इन्हें सँभाल कर न रखना चाहिए था। मैं बड़ी हैरानी में पड़ गयी। पर्चों पर सुपरिण्टेण्डेण्ट के हस्ताक्षर थे और वे पत्र जेल के द्वारा ही आये थे। आज उन्हें रोकने का मतलब क्या था? नियमानुसार पत्र रोकने का इस समय जेलर को कोई हक़ नहीं था, पर जेलर ने बार-बार यही कहा कि—''साहब से पूछ कर पत्र लौटाये जायेंगे।'' मैं बड़ी कठिनता में पड़ गयी। पत्र मिल नहीं रहे थे और मेरा दिल पत्रों को छोड़ घर जाने को चाह नहीं रहा था। ये वही पत्र थे, जिनका मैंने एक धार्मिक पुस्तक के स्वाध्याय की तरह जेल में रोज़ पाठ किया था। मेरे जेलवाले घर की यही तो बहुमूल्य सम्पत्ति थी। जेलर ने कहा, आप फ़िकर न करें, मैं इन्हें सँभाल कर रखूँगा। और यदि साहब आज्ञा दे देंगे, तो आप को भेज दिये जायेंगे, नहीं तो यक़ीन रखें, मैं इन्हें जला दूँगा। अन्ततः मुझे पत्र वहीं छोड़ कर दफ़्तर से बाहर आना पड़ा। पूरे साढ़े ग्यारह बजे जेल का बड़ा फाटक खुला। जेलर ने कहा,''अच्छा मिसेज़ शास्त्री, हमारी ग़लतियाँ माफ़

करना।'' जेलर भी मेरे साथ दरवाज़े तक बाहर आये। द्वार के बाहर एक ताँगा खड़ा था। जेलर ने कहा—''इस ताँगे पर सामान रख कर आप जा सकती हैं।'' एक ताँगा उसी पर पलँग, बक्स, बिस्तर और मैं—सब कैसे जाते? संयोगवश उसी समय शहर की एक गाड़ी आ पहुँची। मैं उसी में बैठ गयी। जेलर ने कहा—''ख़ुदा हाफ़िज़ है।'' मेरी गाड़ी घर की ओर चल दी। रास्ता वही था, जिसे बन्द लॉरी में आठवें दिन हस्पताल जाते हुए कई बार देखा था। पर आज उसमें एक नवीन सुन्दरता और आकर्षण दिखाई देने लगा। मैं बाहर की ओर देख कर सोचती कि क्या सचमुच मैं घर की ओर जा रही हूँ। जेल की तरफ़ से बिस्तर और खाट सहित आती हुई गाड़ी दूसरे लोगों में उत्सुकता पैदा कर रही थी। लोग दुकानों से उचक-उचक कर देखने लगे। कइयों ने पहचाना, एक ने चिल्ला कर कहा—''उर्मिला जी छूट गयीं।'' एक लॉरी में कुछ यात्री चढ़ रहे थे, उन्होंने घूम कर देखा। एक ने कहा—''बहन जी, नमस्ते।'' सीधी सड़क आ जाने से दूर से ही घर का बरामदा दीखने लगा। मैंने देखा, उसमें कुछ लोग खड़े हैं। बरामदे पर दृष्टि पड़ते ही मेरा हृदयः उमड़ने लगा, मानो वह मेरे शरीर से निकल कर आगे बढ़ना चाहता हो। न जाने कितने भावों ने मुझे दबा लिया। मुझे पता न चला कि वह हर्ष था या क्षोभ, चिन्ता थी या उत्सुकता। वह न जाने कौन किस प्रकार का हृदय का अनिर्वचनीय भाग था। मैं क्षण भर के लिए बेसुध हो गयी, स्तब्ध-सी रह गयी, पाँच मिनट बाद मैंने देखा कि मैं उसी कमरे में बैठी हूँ, जहाँ छः मास पूर्व जेल जाने के लिए मेरा सामान तैयार किया जा रहा था।